MY LIFE FOR THE POOR

In the following pages you will read about a world-famous person who is a Nobel Peace Prize recipient, a person who is as busy as a head of government, a person who lacks any secretarial staff primarily because she is unaware of how important she is. A person whose sole desire is to serve the poorest of the poor. A person who through word, deed, and action has touched and encouraged more hearts to love, and with this book will help motivate more hands to serve.

MOTHER TERESA OF CALCUTTA

MY LIFE FOR THE POOR

THE POOR

Mother Teresa
of Calcutta

EDITED BY JOSÉ LUIS GONZÁLEZ-BALADO
AND JANET N. PLAYFOOT

BALLANTINE BOOKS • NEW YORK

Library of Congress Catalog Card Number: 85-42787

ISBN 0-345-33780-8

This edition published by arrangement with Harper & Row, Pub-lishers, Inc.

Manufactured in the United States of America

First Ballantine Books/Epiphany Edition: March 1987

Contents

Preface

BROTHER ANDREW, MC

When José Luis González-Balado and Janet N. Playfoot asked me to write a few words for this book, I delayed and delayed.

It should not be difficult for me to write about Mother Teresa, for she has such an amazing story. Her life is unbelievably rich and full.

In addition, I have had the privilege of sharing closely with her in one of her great initiatives: the growth and expansion of the Missionaries of Charity Brothers which she founded.

She and I know and understand each other well.

And yet I find it difficult to write.

Much has been written about Mother Teresa. It has reached a point where the same things are being written again and again.

In addition, from my own small experience of life, I have come to suspect that the best stories are not— cannot even be—written, especially with people who try to live and serve God and his people.

So with all this in mind, I can appreciate what José

Luis González-Balado and Janet N. Playfoot have done.

In this book, they have allowed Mother Teresa to tell her story in her own words. They have given us the nearest thing we shall probably ever have to an autobiography by Mother Teresa herself.

This, then, is an authentic book. It may not be complete. No book about her could be complete.

And part of its authenticity is the spirit of Mother Teresa that comes through in her own words about it all, which José Luis González-Balado and his wife Janet N. Playfoot have woven together into both a life story and a testament to spirituality.

BROTHER ANDREW, MC

Introduction

T*he readers of this book have the right to know* that it has not all been directly written by Mother Teresa.

We doubt whether Mother Teresa has written much more than short letters to her sisters or to people especially linked in sharing her work of loving service to the poor.

After years of being in touch with her, we have received from Mother Teresa only three or four short letters. Of course, our letters to her have been more frequent and longer, but Mother Teresa has no time to answer. She is as busy as a head of government, but she lacks any secretarial staff—mostly because she is unaware of being so busy, but especially of being so important!

This book has not all been written, but mostly spoken, by Mother Teresa.

What it may have lost in literary correctness, it has undoubtedly gained in freshness and vivacity of style.

Wherever she goes, Mother Teresa is always insistently invited to talk to people who enthusiastically fill churches or big halls to be able to listen to her simple words. Hardly ever does there lack one or even a hundred tape recorders recording that particular atmosphere, that readily familiar voice.

We ourselves have attended some of these meetings with Mother Teresa and heard directly some of her simple and sincere addresses. We have listened and recorded many of her lively answers, in both formal and informal interviews. But we have, as well, a certain amount of cassettes with recordings of Mother Teresa in places where we have never, unfortunately, been and in meetings which we could not attend.

We have exchanged some cassettes with people who were there. And we have received a few more from one person who is a generous collector of documents regarding Mother Teresa. We write her name as an expression of gratitude although knowing that she is not expecting any thanks for her work, done for higher aims rather than for acknowledgement: Alice Grattan-Esmonde.

We have to recall one more name, that of the Czechoslovakian Jesuit and bishop Paul Hnilica. A frequent contributor to the Vatican Radio broadcasts for the Eastern European countries and very familiar with Mother Teresa, he has often interviewed her.

Once, in the early seventies, we had a long talk with him about Mother Teresa in his apartment in Rome. He put at our complete and free disposal, in addition to his personal impressions, all his materials, some of which have made a consistent contribution to this book.

While listening to Mother Teresa's words, we came

to gradually realize that she often tells touching episodes which she has witnessed and lived.

All of them are episodes expressing love for the poorest of the poor, those whom Mother Teresa calls Our People.

We thought they deserved to be collected into an exciting book which Mother Teresa would never have time (or desire!) to write.

Mother Teresa is too busy to write books. She is too humble also.

The anecdotes which Mother Teresa could tell are uncountable. But she always searches for people in order to serve them, not to speak about them.

The anecdotes that Mother Teresa narrates here are a few among thousands and thousands. They are all real, but on her lips and with her intentions, they become symbols or parables.

Quite often, while she tells them, she forgets about their concrete dates. (She says "the other day" or "some weeks back" for events ten or twenty years old.)

She repeats the same anecdotes here and there. Here she tells this detail which she omits there, but the substance never changes: it always keeps its real character, although often reaching parabolic symbolism.

This book is, however, more than a simple collection of anecdotes and episodes. By uniting and linking answers and dates, confidences and talks from Mother Teresa, we have surprisingly arrived at the construction of a kind of authentic autobiography of this extraordinary woman.

Let these pages touch and encourage more hearts

to love and more hands to serve the poor. This will surely happen, with God's grace.

We have undertaken the hard but pleasant task of collecting these materials for this purpose, with this inner sureness.

José Luis González-Balado
Janet N. Playfoot

1. My Family and My Vocation

I *am Albanian by birth. Now I am a citizen of India.* I am also a Catholic nun. In my work, I belong to the whole world. But in my heart, I belong to Christ.

The first time I said I wanted to devote my life to God, my mother opposed me. Then, she said, "All right, my daughter, you go. But be careful to be always of God and Christ, only." Not only God, but also she would have condemned me if I had not followed my vocation with faithfulness. She will ask me one day, "My daughter, have you lived only for God?"

I was still very young, no more than twelve years old, when, in the heart of my family, I first experienced the desire to belong completely to God.

I thought and prayed about it for six years.

At times, I had the impression that my vocation did not exist. But finally I was convinced that God called me.

Our Lady of Letnice interceded for me and helped me to discover it.

In the moments when I was uncertain about my vocation, some advice of my mother's helped me a lot.

She often repeated to me, "When you accept a task, do it willingly. If not, don't accept it!"

Once I asked my confessor for advice about my vocation, I asked, "How can I know if God is calling me and for what he is calling me?"

He answered, "You will know by your happiness. If you are happy with the idea that God calls you to serve him and your neighbor, this will be the proof of your vocation. Profound joy of the heart is like a magnet that indicates the path of life. One has to follow it, even though one enters into a way full of difficulties."

I often remember my mother and father praying together, every night, with the other members of the family.

Because of his work, my father was often absent from home. But even in those cases we came together every night around our mother to pray with her.

Our most frequent prayer in those cases was the holy rosary.

It was at the feet of our Lady of Letnice (in Skopje) where I first heard the divine call, convincing me to serve God and to devote myself to his service.

I remember the afternoon of her feast of the Assumption. I was praying with a lighted candle in my hands and singing in my heart, full of joy inside, when I took the decision to wholly devote myself to God through religious life.

I also remember that it was in the sanctuary of our

Lady of Letnice in Skopje where I heard the voice of God calling me to be all his by consecrating myself to him and to the service of my neighbors.

For some time it had been a wish that I had carried hidden in my heart.

I still remember those beautiful times and some of the hymns that we sang to our Lady, especially the one entitled *Në Cëernagore kem nji Nanë* (In the Black Mountain we've a mother).

A few years ago, I was able to return to Skopje and to Letnice. I felt very happy kneeling again in front of the image of our Lady to pray to her. The habit of the image had changed but the eyes and her look continued to be the same after so many years. With my prayer I wanted to give thanks to God for the past years from the first time I had left Skopje. They were fruitful years, and if I had to begin again, I would leave Skopje to take the same path.

I found Skopje very changed, but it continued to be my Skopje, where I had spent my childhood with my family and where I was happy.

We opened a house of the Missionaries of Charity in Skopje. This filled me with happiness. Establishing a small community of Missionaries of Charity in the town where I was born showed my gratitude and that of the sisters to God and to my place of birth.

In my address to the people of Skopje I said, "The sisters are the present that I make to my village. I hope that Skopje gives more vocations to the church so that we can offer more sisters. I always carry in my heart the people of Skopje and Albania. I ask God that his peace descend over all the hearts of all their inhabitants and over those of all the world."

A Very Happy Family

We were a very happy family.

We were very closely united, especially after my father's death.

We lived for each other and we made each other's lives very full and very happy.

I have never forgotten my mother.

She used to be very busy the whole day, but as soon as the evening came, she moved very quickly to get ready to meet my father.

At the time, we didn't understand. We used to smile, we used to laugh, we used to tease her. Now, I remember what a tremendous, delicate love she had for him.

It didn't matter what happened: she was ready there with a smile to meet him.

My mother was a holy woman.

She imparted to all her children that love for God and that love for her neighbor.

She brought us up very closely, in the love of Jesus. She herself prepared us for our first communion, and so we learned to love God above all things from our mother.

My Wish to Become a Missionary

I was only twelve years old, no more, and lived at home with my parents in Skopje (Yugoslavia) when I felt for the first time the desire to become a nun.

I went to a non-Catholic school but there were good priests who helped boys and girls to follow their vocation, according to God's call.

It was then that I realized that my vocation was towards the poor.

But between twelve and eighteen years of age I forgot this desire to become a nun.

I'll repeat: we were a very happy family.

At eighteen years, I decided again to leave home to become a missionary.

From then on, I have never had the least doubt of my decision.

It was the will of God: he made the choice.

Some Jesuit missionaries went to India while I was still at home.

They used to send word to us of what they were doing for the people there.

They used to give us the most beautiful descriptions about the experiences they had with the people and especially with the children in India.

They made the contact for me with the Loreto Sisters who were working in India at that time.

Through these Jesuit missionaries, I came into contact with the Loreto Sisters and joined them in Rathfarnham, Dublin.

THE HAPPIEST NUN IN THE WORLD

Following my vocation was a sacrifice which Christ asked me and my people, since we were a very happy and united family.

But I didn't leave home until I was eighteen.

Even after so many years, I still remember when I went to the mother house of the Loreto Sisters in Rathfarnham.

A few months ago, I saw the places where I had been as a young postulant. I still remember the community room and chapel, everything.

I left Rathfarnham after only six weeks. I had joined in October 1928 and in January I went to India to do the noviciate in 1929.

I did my noviciate in Darjeeling and took the vows with the Loreto Sisters.

For twenty years, I was at work in education in the St. Mary's High School, which was mostly for middle-class children. (There were some of the better-class people also.) That was the only Catholic high school that we had in Calcutta at the time. (I can't say whether I was a good teacher. This my pupils would know better. But I loved teaching.)

In Loreto I was the happiest nun in the world.

To leave the work that I carried out there was a great sacrifice.

What I didn't leave was my condition of being a nun.

The change was only in the work.

My Sisters of Loreto were limited to teaching, which is an authentic apostolate for Christ.

It was a call within the call: something like a second vocation.

It was the inner command to renounce Loreto, where I was very happy, to go to serve the poor in the streets.

In 1946, while I was going by train to Darjeeling for my spiritual retreat, I again experienced a call to renounce everything and to follow Christ into the slums, to serve the poorest of the poor.

I understood that God wanted something from me.

My Belonging to Christ

In 1948, twenty years after I came to India, I actually decided upon this close contact with the poorest of the poor. It was for me a special vocation to give all to belong to Jesus.

I felt that God wanted from me something more. He wanted me to be poor with the poor and to love him in the distressing disguise of the poorest of the poor.

I had the blessing of obedience.

Once I represented the matter to my superiors and to the bishop of Calcutta, they felt that it was God's will, that God wanted it. I had their blessing, the blessing of obedience.

With that, there is no doubt or mistake. Maybe it looks a failure, but if it's a failure, it's only in the eyes of people, not in the eyes of God.

I didn't have to give up anything: vocation is belonging to Christ, and my belonging to him had not changed.

I was only changing the means to serve the poorest of the poor.

The work is only a way to put our love for Christ into action.

(The vocation itself, my belonging to Christ, didn't have to change. It had rather deepened.)

My love for Christ had deepened by making that big sacrifice. That's why I call it a simple *call within a call*.

My vocation was a continuation of my belonging to Christ and of my being only his.

At the same time, some of the girls whom I was

teaching and who visited the poor in the slums and the sick in the hospital, expressed the desire of becoming nuns so that they could devote themselves fully to the apostolate among the very poor.

It was on the tenth of September 1946, in the train that took me to Darjeeling, the hill station in the Himalayas, that I heard the call of God.

In quiet, intimate prayer with our Lord, I heard distinctly, a call within a call.

The message was quite clear: I was to leave the convent and help the poor whilst living among them. It was an order. I knew where I belonged, but I did not know how to get there.

I felt intensely that Jesus wanted me to serve him among the poorest of the poor, the uncared for, the slum dwellers, the abandoned, the homeless. Jesus invited me to serve him and follow him in actual poverty, to practise a kind of life that would make me similar to the needy in whom he was present, suffered and loved.

≪≪≪≪≪≪≪≪≪≪≪≪≪≪≪≪≪≪≪≪≪≪≪≪≪≪≪≪≪≪≪

2. The Missionaries of Charity

I *left the Loreto Sisters in 1948.*

On my first trip along the streets of Calcutta after leaving the Sisters of Loreto, a priest came up to me. He asked me to give a contribution to a collection for the Catholic press. I had left with five rupees, and I had given four of them to the poor. I hesitated, then gave the priest the one that remained. That afternoon, the same priest came to see me and brought an envelope. He told me that a man had given him the envelope because he had heard about my projects and wanted to help me. There were fifty rupees in the envelope. I had the feeling, at that moment, that God had begun to bless the work and would never abandon me.

ONLY YOU, MY GOD!

I didn't have any difficulty with the sisters when I left Loreto.

They were all most understanding and cooperative.

9

However, to leave Loreto was my greatest sacrifice, the most difficult thing I have ever done. It was much more difficult than to leave my family and country to enter religious life.

Loreto meant everything to me. In Loreto I had received my spiritual training. I had become a religious there. I had given myself to Jesus in the Institute. I liked the work, teaching the girls.

Really, I insist, to leave Loreto was much more difficult for me than leaving my family when I entered the convent. Of course, I didn't run away from the convent to obtain more freedom.

Soon after leaving Loreto, I was on the street, with no shelter, no company, no helper, no money, no employment, no promise, no guarantee, no security.

Then I prayed, "My God, you, only you. I trust in your call, your inspiration. You will not let me down."

I needed a roof to shelter the abandone so I started to search.

I walked and walked all the time, until I couldn't walk any more.

Then, I understood better the exhaustion of the really poor, always in search of a little food, of medicines, of everything.

The memory of the material security that I enjoyed in the convent of Loreto came then to me as a temptation and I prayed like this:

"O God, through free choice and through your love, I want to stay here and do your will. No, I cannot go back. My community are the poor. Their security is mine. Their health is my health. My home is the home of the poor: not just of the poor, but of those who are the poorest of the poor. Of those to whom one tries not to get too close for fear of catching something, for fear of the dirt, or because they are covered in germs and disease. Of those that do not go to pray because they can't leave their houses naked. Of those that no longer eat because they haven't the strength. Of those that fall in the streets, knowing that they are going to die, while the living walk by their sides ignoring them. Of those who no longer cry, because they have no tears left. Of the untouchables."

I was sure that the Lord wanted me to be where I was.

I was sure he would offer me a solution.

"ARE YOU PREPARED?"

In March 1949, on the feast of St. Joseph, there was a knock at my door.

I opened it and stood motionless. My heart beat faster as I looked at the frail figure facing me and heard her say, "Mother, I have come to join you."

"It will be a hard life. Are you prepared for it?" I asked the girl.

"I know it will be hard; I am prepared for it," said the girl. And she stepped in.

Then I turned to our Lord, and thanked him: "Dear Jesus, how good you are. So you are sending them! You keep the promise you made me. Lord Jesus, thank you for your goodness."

The first sisters to join were students that I had taught in Loreto.

One by one, I saw young girls arrive after 1949.

They were my students. They wanted to give everything to God, and they were in a hurry to do it.

They took off their expensive saris with great satisfaction in order to put on our humble cotton ones.

They came fully aware of the difficulties.

When a girl who belongs to a very old caste comes to place herself at the service of the outcasts, we are talking about a revolution, the biggest one, the hardest of all: the revolution of love!

THE FIRST TWELVE SISTERS

I took the vows of the new congregation—poverty, chastity, obedience, and charity.

The first group was about twelve, by the time the congregation was established.

With total faith in God's help, protection, and goodness, I prayed to our Lord from my deepest heart:

"Father, glorify your son that your Son may return the glory to you, Father glorify your Son, let him be glorified through your unworthy instruments, for it is for him, for his glory that we are here, that we work and suffer and pray. All we do is for Jesus. Our life has no meaning if it is not all for him. Let men know him, and thus come to possess the eternal life he brought us.

"Eternal life, Father, is to know you, the one true God, and Jesus Christ, whom you have sent.

"May we bring this eternal life to the poor, deprived as they are of all comfort, of material possessions; may they come to know you, love you, possess you, share in your life, you who are the God and

Father of men and of my Lord Jesus Christ, source of all truth and goodness and happiness.

"May we bring to you those we meet, those for whom we work, those who help us, those who die in our hands, those we receive as Jesus received the children he blessed, the sick he cured, the sufferers he befriended.

"Father, I pray you for these sisters, whom you have chosen to serve you and belong to you. They were yours, and you gave them to me. You want me to lead them to you. You wish them to be an image of your Son, your own perfect image, that men may believe that you have sent him. That seeing their works, men may acknowledge that Christ was sent by you.

"You gave them to me, and I bring them to you.

"You took them away from the world and its spirit, that they may live in the world as the brides of Jesus, neither belonging to the world nor following its corrupt ways.

"Holy Father, I pray for them that they may be dedicated to your holy name, sanctified to you, reserved for your service, immolated to you in sacrifice. To this end I consecrate myself to you, I dedicate myself as your victim with Jesus Christ, the victim of the sacrifice.

"Father so good, I pray not only for these my sisters, but for all those who will come to join them and those who through them will be drawn to you and believe in you.

"Father, grant that my sisters may all be one, as you and Jesus are one, that they may live through your spirit.

"That the love with which you loved us may be in them and that Jesus may be in them."

CARRIERS OF GOD'S LOVE

Since then, girls from all over the world have been joining.

We are getting hundreds of wonderful young vocations.

The young people, in their application, write something very beautiful: "I want a life of poverty, prayer and sacrifice that will lead me to the service of the poor."

In 1950 the Holy Father approved of the new congregation of the Missionaries of Charity.

I didn't choose this name, Missionaries of Charity. It came from the call.

It is what we are meant to be: carriers of God's love, as the sisters are called in Yemen, a Moslem country. (We are the only Christians there.)

The people of the place call them carriers of God's love, because they do this humble work with so much joy, with so much inner happiness.

I had decided that we should eat rice and salt like the very poor of Calcutta.

But the medical missionaries of Patna said I was to feed my sisters well, and I have followed their advice.

Mother Dengel, the superior of the medical missionary sisters of Patna, said to me with great energy, "If you make your sisters do that, eat only rice and salt, you will commit a serious sin. Within a short time, those young girls will fall a prey to tuberculosis and die. How do you expect your sisters to work, if their bodies receive no sustenance? The very poor work very little, become sick and die young. Do you want your nuns to suffer that fate? Or do you wish them to be strong and able to labor for Christ?"

Mother Dengel also added, "You must feed your sisters well. They will have much work, and move among the sick in unhealthy localities. To resist disease, they must be well fed."

The majority of our sisters are from India. (We are really an Indian congregation.) But in Rome we have a noviciate with novices from sixteen nationalities, from Europe and America.

We also have a noviciate in Australia, and have recently opened a new noviciate in Africa, as we are getting quite a lot of good vocations there also.

We have high-, middle- and ordinary-class girls, and that's the most beautiful thing about these young girls, so fully dedicated and determined to give their all to Christ. They are all very anxious to live a life of poverty. (For us, this is very important: if we really want to know the poor, we must know what poverty is. It is why in our society, poverty is our freedom and our strength.)

The Missionaries of Charity do firmly believe that they are touching the body of Christ in his distressing disguise whenever they are helping and touching the poor.

We cannot do this with a long face.

We cannot do it just anyhow, because it is to Jesus that we are doing it.

The whole of our society is engaged in doing just that: feeding the hungry Christ, clothing the naked

Christ, taking care of the sick Christ, and giving a home to the homeless Christ.

It is very beautiful to see our young people so fully devoted, so full of love for God's poor!

FOUR CONDITIONS TO BECOME A MC

The generous surrender of our young sisters is a most wonderful gift of God to our society and to the whole church.

It is not the excitement of the work that is drawing them. It is something much deeper and more wonderful.

Many of our sisters come from well-to-do families. To see them just leave their life behind is something wonderful.

To be able to understand the poor, to be able to understand the poverty of Christ, we choose to be poor. Many times we just choose not to have things that we could easily have, but we freely choose not to have them.

We joyfully accept to spend twenty-four hours with the kind of people with whom sometimes we cannot even converse properly.

They are the poorest of the poor, covered with dirt and with maggots.

They are the lepers, the abandoned destitute, the homeless, the sick, the dying.

It is wonderful to see the joy and the greatness of love in these young sisters.

It is a living miracle that impresses hundreds of people, even non-Christians, who come close to them.

All our sisters are full of joy. They are the most striking example of living faith with joy.

We try to teach them, from the very beginning, to pray while working, doing it for Jesus and doing it to Jesus.

This brings a tremendous closeness with him.

This helps us to be in love with Jesus and to find him in the distressing disguise of the poorest of the poor as we find him in the appearance of bread in the Eucharist.

A young girl wishing to join our society must meet the four conditions that are required to be a Missionary of Charity. She must be healthy of mind and body. She must have ability to learn. She must have plenty of common sense and a cheerful disposition.

If she meets these four conditions, then she comes and sees the work (like in the gospel, when our Lord said, "Come and see").

She goes to one of our houses and comes into close contact with the poor, with the people, with the sisters. She works with them, prays with them, stays with them.

Then, she decides if this is what God wants from her.

If she joins, then she spends six months as an aspirant, six months as a postulant and two years as a novice.

After this, there are six years of temporary vows. Then, one year before final vows, she comes back again to the noviciate to deepen her spiritual life, because we are not social workers: we are trying to live a contemplative life by spreading the love and compassion of Jesus in the world by doing the work of salvation.

As a rule, the age of seventeen is the youngest we accept girls applying to join our society.

As I said before, we have six months for a girl to "come and see." (We call it this, but it is what used to be called aspirancy.)

We try to put the gospel's words into life.

Then we have six months of postulancy and two years of noviciate. And then, six years of temporary vows.

One year before temporary vows end, the girls come back to the noviciate for a third year with more intense spiritual life and deeper oneness with Christ. Before they come for the tertianship, as we call it, they go home for a fortnight to decide, "Is this what I want to have for life?"

They go back to their parents for a fortnight. Then they decide if they really want to take the final vows.

We have very few girls who leave: only those girls who don't meet the four conditions listed above. (Some of them become ill before they are professed.)

They don't leave because our life is hard. Not at all. Up to now, only a few have stayed back, and most of them for family reasons. Otherwise, God has been very good to us.

A MISSION OF LOVE

Ours is a mission of love.

We are there to bring Christ to the people and to bring the people to Christ.

A Missionary of Charity is a person who is sent. Being Missionaries of Charity, we are sent to bring God's love, to prove God's love: that God loves the world, that God loves the poor. He shows his love through us for them.

We show our love for God by putting our love for him into living action through serving the poorest of the poor.

It is an exchange between God and us. God uses us to show his love for the poor through our dedication and consecration to him.

We use his love to prove to the people our love for God in action through our service to the poorest of the poor—be they the lepers or the dying, the crippled, the unloved, or the uncared for. Whoever they may be, for us they are Christ in the distressing disguise of the poorest of the poor.

I remember one of our sisters who had just come from the university. She came from a well-to-do family.

As we have in our rules, the very next day after the girls have joined the society, they go to the Home for the Dying.

Before they went, I told them, "You saw the priest during Mass: with what love, with what delicate care he touched the body of Christ! Make sure you do the same thing when you go to the Home, for Jesus is there in the distressing disguise."

And they went.

After three hours, they came back and one of them, the girl who had come from the university, who had seen so much, so many things, came to my room with such a beautiful smile on her face. She said,

"For three hours I have been touching the body of Christ."

And I said, "What did you do, what happened?"

She said, "They brought a man from the street, covered with maggots. And I knew, though I found it very difficult, I knew that I was touching the body of Christ."

Some time ago, in Bombay, our sisters picked up a man from the street. In lifting him up, the whole of his back remained on the street.

They brought him home: cleaned him, washed him, but the man never said a word.

After a few hours, after giving him a bath, there was nothing you could see, apart from all the bones on his back.

Then I asked the sisters, "What did you feel when you were touching him?"

One of the sisters answered my question in the name of the others, "I have never felt the presence of Christ so real, Mother, as when I was touching him."

A DROP IN THE OCEAN

Since I believe that God is giving me vocations, he means me to use them, not to keep them.

In all the places where we are, we are invited either by the bishop or whoever is the head, or by the government.

In Rome we were invited by the Holy Father Paul VI himself.

Lately, the last group that went to Mexico were invited by the president himself. But in Guatemala I sent the sisters as a gift of love from India to serve the people who had been so wounded by the earthquake. Otherwise, in all the places we are always asked to come.

I will never forget one day when I went to one of our houses and found the community very badly disturbed.

I couldn't understand. So I asked the sisters, "Do you have confession? Do you have instruction?"

"No," they answered, "we haven't had it for a long time."

I asked again, "Why?"

"Because the father is very busy," they told me.

I prayed, went to the bishop and said, "Since your priests have no time for my sisters, I am going to remove the sisters from here."

Because that is the only condition I make with the bishops: to take care of our spiritual life, of confession and instruction, holy mass and holy communion.

For the rest, we depend solely on divine providence, and God has always taken care of us.

The whole world: it sounds so big and so much!

One at a time. That one is Jesus. Yes, it is Jesus, because he has said so, "I was hungry and you fed me."

That's why the poor become the hope of salvation for mankind.

We are going to be judged on what we have done to them and how we have accepted them.

The missionary brothers and sisters have taken this into account. I think it has a tremendous influence on them.

They are working to answer the call of the poor of

the world. I think the world today turns its back on the poor and this is turning its back on Christ himself.

What we do is nothing but a drop in the ocean.

But if we didn't do it, the ocean would be one drop less.

We have no reason to be despondent or discouraged or unhappy, because we are doing it to Jesus.

I know that there are thousands and thousands of poor, but I think of only one at a time.

Jesus was only one and I take Jesus at his word.

He has said, "You did it to me. . . ."

My sisters, the brothers, and I, we take one person, one individual person, at a time.

You can save only one at a time. We can love only one at a time.

OUR POVERTY'S OUR FREEDOM

We have absolutely no difficulty regarding having to work in countries with many faiths, like India.

We treat all people as children of God. They are our brothers and sisters. We show great respect to them.

But they know very well that what I have is a treasure that I'd like to give them, and I am not afraid to tell them so. But I also tell them that faith is a gift of God.

Our work is to encourage these Christians and non-Christians to do works of love. And every work of love, done with a full heart, always brings people closer to God.

If they accept God in their lives, then they are a co-worker. If they don't, it's their answer.

This has been a most wonderful gift of God to us. For example, in 1975, when we celebrated our Silver Jubilee, we had eighteen different Religions saying in their own way, with their own worship, *thank you* to God for the Missionaries of Charity; and *thank you* to the people who share the work of the Missionaries of Charity.

It was a most beautiful proof that we all work as one.

More and more people are asking how to help.

We give them a chance to work for love, such as to help somebody in their own family first, and then their next-door neighbor, and then to find the poor around them.

When that contact is made (I never ask for money; I never ask them to give anything to me, but I always ask them to come and see, to come and touch), when that contact has been made, they know what they have to do.

What is very beautiful in the young people is their generosity.

We give them a paper to fill up, and we ask them, "Why do you want to join the Missionaries of Charity?"

Most of them write, "I want a life of poverty, prayer and sacrifice that will lead me to the service of the poor."

Very often we think that the young people are drawn to the work, but you would be surprised that they are drawn to the life of poverty.

Our young people want to give all or nothing.

I could give a very beautiful example of a very rich girl who wrote to me and said, "For many years Jesus is calling me to become a religious. I have tried to see

23

where Jesus wants me to go. I've seen that what they have, I have. If I join them, I won't have to give up anything."

She wanted to give up everything to be free. That's why poverty for us is a freedom, a complete freedom.

WE BELONG TO GOD

Our sisters and brothers want to give God everything.

All they know very well is that it is the Christ the hungry, Christ the homeless, Christ the naked they are serving. And this love is so great that it makes the giving a joy.

That's why they are very happy. They are happy because they feel they have found what they have been looking for.

First of all we try to make our aspirants, postulants and novices understand that poverty—not only poverty of spirit, but material poverty—is freedom.

So, we try to free our sisters from all that is not of Jesus.

When they understand what poverty is, they can grow up spiritually through that faith in Jesus and in the Eucharist.

Our lives are very much woven with the Eucharist. We have a deep faith in Jesus' Blessed Sacrament. Because of this faith, it is not so difficult to see Christ and touch him in the distressing disguise of the poor.

Up to today, no one has ever been rude to our sisters; no one has ever tried to do an evil to them.

Our sari habit is the sign of our consecration to

God, and it is a sign of purity and of our belonging to God.

The rosary in hand has been a tremendous protection, strength, and help.

In New York City and in many other places where there is fighting, suffering, and hatred, our sisters are able to move freely without anybody even touching them.

Even in India, in Calcutta, when we had very difficult days and many people could not go out, our sisters were out all the time, and even people who were anxious and who were doing wrong things helped the sisters to move freely, so that nobody could do them any harm.

I think that the habit they wear has much to do with this; it gets that respect and that love from the people.

Though the people are what they are sometimes, still they know who belongs to God the Lord.

OUR PARTICULAR MISSION

In 1976, at the invitation of the president of Mexico, we opened a house in that country.

Our sisters, as it is accustomed in our society, walk and walk until their legs ache to see which is the worst place, where the need is greatest to begin from.

In Mexico, the poverty of the people was very great. Wherever they visited (it was in the outskirts of Mexico mostly), there was very great poverty.

To the sisters' surprise, nobody asked for clothes,

for medicine, for food. Nothing except, "Teach us the word of God."

It struck me so much! These people are hungry for God: "Teach us the word of God."

I think, quite possibly this is because the sisters have the rosary in hand, as we go anywhere in the world (like in Yemen, where we have gone after eight hundred years).

The sisters walk down the streets with rosary in hand. Our Lady is our mother, and she is also our strength and our protection. (We have a mother in Heaven, Mother Mary, our joy and the cause of our joy.)

All these years, young sisters have entered the most terrible places and up to today no one has ever touched them. Even in New York City, where they say we are in the worst place . . .

We are called the Missionaries of Charity.

God is love. A Missionary of Charity must be a missionary of love. She must be full of charity in her own soul and spread that same charity to the souls of others, Christians and non-Christians.

As Jesus Christ was sent by his Father so he sends us too, filled with his spirit, to preach his gospel of love and compassion to the poorest of the poor all over the world.

It shall be our utmost endeavor to proclaim Jesus Christ to men of all nations, especially to those who are under our care.

Our aim is to quench the infinite thirst of Jesus Christ for love by the profession of the evangelical counsels and by wholehearted free service to the poorest of the poor, according to the teaching and life of our Lord in the gospel, revealing in a unique way the kingdom of God.

Our particular mission is to labor at the salvation and sanctification of the poorest of the poor.

JESUS EXPLAINS OUR LIFE

We are first of all religious.

We are not social workers, not teachers, not nurses or doctors.

We are religious sisters.

We serve Jesus in the poor.

We nurse him, feed him, clothe him, visit him, comfort him in the poor, the abandoned, the sick, the orphans, the dying.

All we do—our prayer, our work, our suffering—is for Jesus. Our life has no other reason or motivation.

This is a point many people do not understand.

I serve Jesus twenty-four hours a day. Whatever I do is for him. And he gives me strength.

I love him in the poor and the poor in him. But always the Lord comes first.

Whenever a visitor comes to our house, I take him to the chapel to pray for a while.

I tell him, "Let us first greet the master of the house. Jesus is here."

It is for him we work, to him we devote ourselves. He gives us the strength to carry on this life and to do so with happiness.

Without him we could not do what we do. We certainly could not continue doing it for a whole lifetime. One year, two years, perhaps; but not during a whole life, without thought of reward, without expectation of anything good except to suffer with him who loved us so much that he gave his life for us.

Without Jesus our life would be meaningless, incomprehensible.

Jesus explains our life.

In the choice of the works of the apostolate of the Missionaries of Charity, there was neither planning nor preconceived ideas.

We started work as needs and opportunities arose.

God showed what he wanted us to do.

One day, we saw alongside the Campbell Hospital, close to our house, a man dying on the roadside.

I inquired. The hospital authorities could not accommodate him.

We went to a drugstore to get some medicine for him.

When we returned with the medicine, the man was dead on the street.

I could not hide my feelings, "They look after a dog or a cat better than a fellow-man. They would not allow that to happen to their pets."

I went to the commissioner of police to complain about this state of affairs. That was the origin of the Kalighat Home for the Dying.

THE KALIGHAT HOME FOR THE DYING

The newspapers in Calcutta publicized the drama of so many people who die on the streets.

I took advantage of the occasion to convince the local authorities.

I said to them, "Just provide me with a roof and I will do the rest."

They assigned me two rooms of the temple of the Goddess Kali, two large rooms, up until then designated as dormitories of the pilgrims.

I accepted them happily as it was a center of Hindu cult devotion.

At once we took our dying and ill there.

The priests of the Goddess Kali didn't look favorably upon our intrusion. But one of them caught a contagious disease and we attended him so well that from then on not only did they stop spying on us, but they became our friends and collaborators.

One morning, as I was washing the patients, a priest of the Kali temple entered the ward. He prostrated himself before me, touched my feet with hands which he then laid on his head.

Then he stood up and said, "For thirty years I have served the Goddess Kali in her temple. Now, the goddess mother stands before me in human form. It is my privilege today to worship the mother present to my eyes."

The question of the Kalighat Home for the Dying was to come up at a Calcutta Corporation meeting.

Some people objected to destitute persons being brought there to die, on religious grounds. They said it defiled the place.

But at the corporation meeting only two members objected on religious grounds.

Nobody offered to provide a better place. So the resolution was passed that we were allowed to remain at Kalighat until a suitable place was found to accommodate the dying.

My friends told me, "Do not worry. The objection has been duly registered and put into cold storage."

In the beginning, the Calcutta Corporation supported the Kalighat Home for the Dying with a monthly subsidy.

One day I informed the corporation that I was no longer in need of their help, and the subsidy was stopped.

At times, the poor we serve arrive in a most terrible state: filthy, covered with sores, eaten up by syphilis. We wash them all. Of course, when a case is really too bad, I do it myself.

Knowing neither their names, nor their place of origin, nor their antecedents, the sisters always treat them all in a loving way.

I always explain to the sisters, "It is Christ you tend in the poor. It is his wounds you bathe, his sores you clean, his limbs you bandage. See beyond appearances, hear the words Jesus pronounced long ago. They are still operative today: *What you do to the least of mine, you do it to me.* When you serve the poor, you serve our Lord Jesus Christ."

THEY CALL US THE "COOLIE SISTERS"

I tell the sisters not to be ashamed when people praise them for what they do. They must let people see what Christ does through us, his humble instruments. It is all to his glory.

I do not want my sisters to perform miracles with unkindness. Rather I prefer them to make mistakes in kindness.

We must work for souls. It is really souls that matter. I feel so happy when I can do good to souls.

I think the sisters also feel happy when they can do good to the souls.

After all, that is why we started looking after the dying, that we might help them think of God in their last moments and make an act of love of God before dying. We want them to die with God.

I think the sisters also see the souls behind the bodies and rejoice when they can do spiritual good.

The work does not distract us from God.

God is good to the institute. The sisters are invited to many places.

We cannot accept all the requests. More sisters are needed. We must pray for vocations.

We carry all our goods ourselves. They call us the coolie sisters, because we always do without porters.

We always sing when sisters leave for new foundations.

I keep in touch with all the houses and all the sisters.

I visit them as often as I can. Of course, my visits become less frequent as the number of foundations increases.

I also write often to the sisters.

Mr. Nehru

When in September 1969 we started our first foundation in Melbourne, some people objected that in a country as rich as Australia, enjoying an advanced social legislation, surely there would be no work for

31

us. There were no slums, no destitute, no people dying on the streets.

So I had to answer them, "What, no work for us? And what about the habitual offenders when they come out of prison, what about their wives and children? What about the drug addicts, the alcoholics, are they not God's children in need of guidance and help?"

When, some years ago, the inauguration of our new children's home in Delhi took place, it was attended by Mr. Nehru.

When the prime minister arrived, accompanied by Mr. Krishna Menon, I said to them, "Let us first go and salute the master of the house."

Then I led them into the chapel where I knelt in prayer.

Mr. Nehru, standing at the back, made a *pranam* with folded hands.

Mr. Krishna Menon went up to the altar to read an inscription and asked me its meaning.

Then we went to sit on the grounds for the inaugural ceremony.

The children garlanded the prime minister and offered him a spiritual bouquet.

I explained that it meant that they had offered prayers and small sacrifices to God to obtain his graces for the prime minister.

Then I asked, "Sir, shall I tell you about our work?"

Mr. Nehru answered me, "No, Mother, you need not tell me about your work. I know about it. That is why I have come."

THE POOR HAVE NO FANS!

We remain very human. We have our ups and downs.

We lose very few sisters. In fact you could count those who have left on the fingers of a single hand, and you would not even need all the fingers.

Last year three left. The superior of one of our houses went away with the parish priest who was the spiritual director of the convent.

I went to see the archbishop of the place who told me he knew this priest had his own ways. I answered him, "Your Grace, if you knew he was not reliable, why did you put him in charge of our sisters?"

Pray for all those who have been in the society that God may protect them and keep them in his love.

Some people would advise me to change certain things. For instance, they tell me that the sisters should have fans in the common room or in the chapel.

I do not want them to have fans. The poor whom they are to serve have no fans.

Most of the girls come from village homes where they had no fans. They should not be more comfortable here than at home. The same is true for the routine of the house.

I always ask these people, "Please do not interfere!"

I was at a meeting of the Superiors General in Europe.

They talked only of changing the structures of society, organizing things in a different way.

It all came to nothing. It did not do something for the poor, or preach Christ to those without religion, to those totally ignorant of God.

I was happy when it was all over. They insisted on my going there, but I felt like a fish out of water.

Once at a meeting in Bangalore, a sister attacked me for distributing food freely to the poor.

She said that I spoiled the poor by my acts of charity.

I answered her, "If I spoil the poor, you and the other sisters spoil the rich in your select schools. And almighty God is the first to spoil us. Does he not give freely to all of us? Then why should I not imitate my God and give freely to the poor what I have received freely?"

She had nothing to answer.

My Budget

We Missionaries of Charity have the responsibility of using whatever gifts we receive according to the intention of the donor—the poorest of the poor we serve.

Let us not spoil the beautiful gift God has given us, the poorest of the poor; let us serve him with love and care.

Money, I never think of it. It always comes. The Lord sends it.

We do his work. He provides the means.

If he does not give us the means, that shows that he does not want the work. So why worry?

One day, Mr. Thomas, the chairman of Hindustan Lever, came to offer a property in Bombay.

He first asked me, "Mother, how is your work financed?"

I answered him, "Mr. Thomas, who sent you here?"

"I felt an urge inside me," he said.

"Well, other people like you come to see me and say the same. That is my budget," I said.

I hope you are not giving only your surplus. You must give what costs you, make a sacrifice, go without something you like, that your gift may have value before God. Then you will be truly brothers and sisters to the poor who are deprived of even the things they need.

I want the gifts to be given not from the giver's abundance, but rather they should be the spontaneous giving of those who are not afraid to love until it hurts.

Giving need not be confined to money or material gifts, but I would like more people to give their hands to serve and their hearts to love—to recognise the poor in their own homes, towns and countries, and to reach out to them in love and compassion.

The International Association of Co-Workers is an opportunity for lay people to grow in the likeness of Christ through humble works of love and service in their own families first, their next door neighbors in the city in which they live, and in the world.

Thus they share in the spirit of our society, and with the Missionaries of Charity.

They become carriers of God's love and compassion.

I believe that God loves the world today through us and all who share their work with us.

To Share with the Poor

We are not a fund-raising group nor are we begging people to give us money.

Let us raise money of love, beginning in the place where we are, with the people with whom we are the closest, and then spread out.

Let us protect this work, this mission, from anything that will make people think that we are raising money.

We do not want people to give from their abundance.

We are giving opportunity to people to love others. It is a chance given to them.

I would like more people to give their hands to serve and their hearts to love—to recognize the poor in their own homes, towns, and countries and to reach out to them in love and compassion, giving where it is most needed.

We should have the joy and freedom of poverty and share the joy of loving.

We are given much, we use much.

We live one day at a time relying on divine providence.

We experience the joy of the freedom of poverty.

We want to feel the joy of sharing.

We must be strictly careful of the mind of the donors and of our poor people.

Giving must generate joy.

Being a co-worker is sharing with the people next door.

Share, as the mother of a starving Hindu family did, who, when we took her some food, immediately took half of it to the hungry Muslims next door.

I went to Mexico. We have opened a house there.

When the sisters go around, the poor do not ask them for clothes, do not ask them for food; they ask them, "Teach us the word of God."

The people don't ask to *hear,* they ask the sisters to *teach* them the word of God.

The president himself made arrangements for our house there, not the government. Everything is well arranged.

Mexico is a huge city. On the outskirts where they gather all the garbage brought by the conservancy department, some five hundred families live on the picking and sorting of refuse, as many people do here in Calcutta.

I told the president to leave them to that work, that is what they can do. Make the surroundings better and improve the houses and let them go on with that work.

Already the sisters have started instructing the children for their first communion.

We shall buy five hundred New Testaments and distribute them to these families. The whole Bible is too expensive. Also it is too difficult for them.

Is this not wonderful that the people are hungry for the word of God? Of course, in Mexico Catholics have been persecuted; this may be the result.

Even now, priests and nuns are not allowed to wear clerical or religious dress. Our sisters go about in their habits—nobody knows what the sari is. But they wear their crosses.

Our Lord and the Eucharist

Christ affirmed that he was present in the Eucharist when he said, "Take and eat, this is my body that will be given up for you. Take and drink of this chalice of my blood that will be shed for you. Do this in memory of me."

I have no difficulty in believing in the real presence of our Lord in the Blessed Eucharist.

The fathers of the church unanimously teach the reality of the presence of Christ. The Council of Trent declares most forcefully, "Christ is present truly, really and substantially in the Eucharist."

Why then do some young priests shake the belief of our people by saying that, after the Mass, there is no real presence in the tabernacle? What do they teach them in some seminaries, nowadays?

A newly ordained priest was sent to give an instruction to the sisters. I was present. The priest laughed at a number of our traditional beliefs.

He said there was no need to genuflect before the Blessed Sacrament when you come to the chapel outside the time of Mass, for the presence of Christ was limited to the time of Mass and communion. He also attacked the idea of religious obedience and ridiculed our traditional devotions.

He spoke in that vein for a whole hour. When he had finished, I led him to the door, thanked him and told him he need not come here any more.

Then I returned to the hall and told the sisters, "You have just heard what a young priest without experience said. They are his ideas and those of a small group. Now I shall tell you what is the traditional teaching of the Church."

And for one hour I refuted all he had said.

How is it that nowadays all over the world so many priests and nuns abandon their calling? Were they not chosen by Christ? Did they not commit themselves to follow him after long and mature reflection? How then can a nun pronounce perpetual vows, and some years later give up the religious life? Are married people not bound to remain faithful to each other until death? Then, why should the same rule not apply to priests and nuns?

In Rome, our sisters are doing a wonderful job. They visit the houses of the poor. They wash and sweep, tidy, mend, and cook for those unable to do so.

They found an old man who must have been well off in earlier days. He lived all alone.

As he was sick, the sisters did all the work for him. One day he told them, "Sisters, you have brought God here; now, bring the priest also."

They brought a priest who heard his confession. (The old man had not confessed his sins for sixty years.) The next day he died in the peace of the Lord.

I told this story in the United States at a meeting they had asked me to address. After the meeting, a priest came to me and said: "I had decided to leave the priesthood and sent my letter of resignation to my bishop. After hearing what you said, I shall cancel my resignation and remain at the service of souls as a priest of Christ."

Joy and Prayer

One day a novice in Rome came to me. She was crying.

I asked her, "What is the matter?"

She had just come back from a family and said, "Mother, I have never seen such suffering. They had nothing in the house. There was this terrible sickness, the terrible cancer, and I could do nothing. Please allow me to do a little bit of extra penance. I want to share in that suffering."

She was a young sister, scarcely three years in our congregation, but it was painful for her to see the suffering of the others.

Joy is prayer. Joy is strength. Joy is love. Joy is a net of love by which you can catch souls. God loves a cheerful giver. He gives most who gives with joy. The best way to show our gratitude to God and the people is to accept everything with joy. A joyful heart is the normal result of a heart burning with love. Never let anything so fill you with sorrow as to make you forget the joy of Christ risen.

This I tell my sisters. This I tell to you.

Saying Yes to Jesus

I also tell my sisters:

"Let us not love in words but let us love until it hurts. It hurt Jesus to love us: he died for us. And today it is your turn and my turn to love one another as Jesus loved us. Do not be afraid to say yes to Jesus."

Faithfulness to the little things will help us to grow in love. We have all been given a lighted lamp and it is for us to keep it burning.

We can keep it burning only if we keep on pouring oil inside.

That oil comes from our acts of love.

So, let us keep that lamp burning, so that when Christ comes he will know us.

He will know not only you and me, but all those people we have come in contact with.

He will find himself in all of them, because of the love they have received and the love they have given.

My dear sisters, we must give Jesus full power and possession in our homes.

Once we have Jesus with us, then we can give him to others.

·Don't drift from the humble works. Every work of love is a work of peace, no matter how small it is.

There is so much hatred and hurt! We will not overcome this with fighting, or with bombs; not with things that hurt, but with things that will bring love, joy, and peace.

I believe Saint Vincent de Paul used to tell the young aspirants, "Remember, the poor are our masters: love and obey them."

If we go to the poor with that longing to give God to them, to bring the joy of Jesus which is our strength, I think the world will be soon full of peace and full of love.

The sisters are doing the small things like helping the children, visiting the lonely, the sick, the unwanted.

In one of the houses the sisters visited, a woman living alone was dead many days before she was found, and she was found because her body had begun to decompose. The people around her did not even know her name.

When someone tells me that the sisters have not started any big work, that they are quietly doing small things, I say that even if they helped one person, that was enough. Jesus would have died for one person, for one sinner.

SOMETHING BEAUTIFUL FOR GOD

I'll never forget the time an atheist came to our Home for the Dying in Calcutta.

Just before he arrived, some people had brought a man from the street. (He must have been picked up from a drain, because he was covered with maggots.)

There was a sister who didn't know she was being watched: the way she was touching him, the way she was watching him, and the way she was smiling at him.

I happened to be in the Home for the Dying at that time.

This man stood there, watching the sister and then he came back to me and said, "I came here godless. I came here full of hatred. I am going full of God. I have seen God's love in action. I have seen that through those hands of that sister, through her face, through her tenderness, so full of love for that man. Now I believe."

(I did not know who he was. Surely, I did not know he was an atheist, as he said.)

I'll always repeat: our lives are very much woven with the Eucharist, to be able to see Christ in the poorest of the poor.

That's why we always begin our day with meditation, Mass, and holy communion.

We begin the day at 4:30 in the morning, with prayer and meditation. (Our community is very closely woven together, so we do everything together: we pray together, we eat together, we work together.) We begin with Mass, holy communion, meditation.

Then, since we each have only two saris, we have to wash one every day.

By 7:30, some of the sisters go to the Home for the Dying, some go to work with lepers, some go to the little schools that we have in the slums, some go to prepare food, some go to families, some to teach catechism, and so on.

They spread all over the city. (In Calcutta alone, we have fifty-nine centers: the Home for the Dying is just one of them.) They spread all over the city with the rosary in hand. It is the way for us to pray with the rosary in the street; we do not go to the people without praying; the rosary has been our strength and our protection.

All over the world, we dress as I do and we always go in twos.

We come back at 12:30 and then we have lunch. Then we often have to do housework. Then, for half an hour every sister goes to rest, because all the time they are on their feet. After lunch, we have examination of conscience and say the divine office and the stations of the cross.

By 2:00 we have spiritual reading for half an hour, then have a cup of tea.

At 3:00 the professed sisters go out again. Novices and postulants remain in the house. They have classes of theology and scripture and other things, like constitutions.

Between 6:15 and 6:30 everybody comes back home. From 6:30 to 7:30 we have adoration with the Blessed Sacrament exposed. To be able to have this hour of adoration, we have not had to cut down the work. We work ten hours, twelve hours without having to cut back our service to the poor.

At 7:30 we have dinner. After dinner, for about twenty minutes, we prepare the work for next morning.

From 8:30 until 9:00, we have recreation. (Everybody talks at the top of her voice because all day we have been working.)

At 9:00 we go for night prayers and preparation of meditation for next morning.

Once a week, every week, we have a day of recollection, and that day, the first-year novices go out, because they are the ones who don't go every day. All the professed sisters stay in for the day of recollection. This is a very beautiful time when we can regain all our strength to fill up the emptiness again. That's why it is very beautiful!

That day we have our confessions and adoration.

The work that we Missionaries of Charity are doing is only a means to put our love for Christ in a loving, in a living action.

It is so beautiful that we complete each other!

What we are doing in the slums, maybe you cannot do.

What you are doing in the level where you are called—in your family life, in your college life, in your work—we cannot do.

But you and we together are doing something beautiful for God.

3. My Wonderful Co-workers

MY THREE SECOND SELVES

I have three second selves directing groups of helpers who work on behalf of our institute. These form three branches: the co-workers, the sick and suffering, and the contemplatives.

The co-workers are directed by Mrs. Ann Blaikie in England. They are forty thousand lay persons. Fourteen thousand in the U.K., six thousand in the U.S., some hundred in Belgium, France, Germany, Austria, Sweden, Switzerland, Australia, Italy, Spain, and so on.

They meet regularly. They pray for us. They also prepare bandages and clothes, and other things we need for the dispensaries, for poor children.

What matters is that they work for God.

In several places they have started organizing holy hours for our work. They have meditation, prayer.

At the co-workers' meetings, I always tell them to practise charity first in the home, then among neighbors, then in their locality, in their country, and finally in the world.

But first have a home where there is love and understanding. Love between the members of the family will bring happiness.

I recently went to a meeting of the Calcutta co-workers.

I told them, "Holiness is not a luxury; you are all invited to it."

I said this to Hindus, Moslems, Jains, Parsees, Christians.

They seemed pleased to hear it. I developed the theme in this way. Holiness is to love God and love men. It is therefore not a luxury reserved for a few favored persons. All are invited to be holy.

I told them also that the sisters need their prayers to be able to do their work. That the poor need their help, their understanding, their love.

We all have much to give, to share, to contribute wherever we find ourselves to be living.

Holiness starts in the home, by loving God and those around us for his sake.

JACQUELINE DE DECKER

Then, after the co-workers, there are the sick and suffering, eight hundred of them, I think, organized by Miss Jacqueline de Decker, my second self.

She worked for some time in India. Now she is in Belgium. She underwent seventeen operations.

Some time ago she wrote to me, "You are going to

receive a great favor from our Lord, because of late my pains have increased."

She offers her sufferings for the work of the Missionaries of Charity.

Miss de Decker has organized several hundred sick persons who also offer their pains for the success of the sisters' work.

I met Jacqueline de Decker at the Patna Holy Family Hospital where I stayed after leaving the Loreto Convent.

Miss de Decker wished to work with us, and join our religious institute, but her ill health would not permit it and she was forced to return to Belgium after a stay of two years in India.

Soon after Jacqueline got back to Belgium, in 1952, I wrote her a letter saying this:

"Today I am going to tell you something which I am sure will make you very happy. Why not become spiritually bound to our society? While we work in the slums, etc., you share in the merit, the prayers and the work with your sufferings and prayers. The work is tremendous and I need workers, it is true, but I need souls like yours to pray and suffer for the work. Would you like to become my sister and become a Missionary of Charity, in Belgium in body, but in soul in India, in the world, where there are souls longing for our Lord; but for want of someone to pay the debt for them, they cannot move towards him. You will be a true Missionary of Charity and you will pay their debt, while the sisters—your sisters—help them to come to God, in body.

"Pray over this and let me know what is your

desire. I need many people like you—who would join the society like this—for I want to have: 1) A glorious society in heaven; 2) the suffering society on earth—the spiritual children; 3) and the militant society; the sisters on the battlefield. I am sure you would be very happy to see the sisters fighting the devil in the field of souls. They count nothing as too hard when there is a question of souls. Our Lord must love you much to give you so great a part in his suffering. You are the happy one, for you are his chosen one. Be brave and cheerful and offer much for me—that I may bring many souls to God. Once you come in touch with souls, the thirst grows daily."

Jacqueline was very generous and the first group of sick and suffering co-workers was formed.

Then I wrote to Jacqueline de Decker and to them all other letters, like this one:

"I am happy you are willing to join the suffering members of the Missionaries of Charity. You and all the sick and suffering will share in all our prayers and works and whatever we do for souls, and you do the same with your prayers and sufferings.

"You see, the aim of the society is to satiate the thirst of Jesus on the cross for the love of souls, by working for the salvation and sanctification of the poor in the slums. Who could do better than you and the others who suffer like you? Your suffering and prayers will be the chalice in which we the working members will pour the love of souls we gather around. Therefore you are just as important and necessary as we are for the fulfillment of our aim—to satiate the thirst of Jesus we must be a chalice, and you and the others, men, women, children, old and young, poor and rich, are welcome to make the chalice.

"One thing we must have in common is the spirit of our society: total surrender to God, loving trust, and perfect cheerfulness. Everyone and anyone who wishes to become a Missionary of Charity is welcome, but I want especially the paralysed, the crippled, the incurables to join, for they will bring many souls to the feet of Jesus (. . .)

"My very dear children, let us love Jesus with our whole heart and soul. Let us bring him many souls. Keep smiling. Smile at Jesus in your suffering—for to be a real MC you must be a cheerful victim. What a beautiful vocation is ours: to be carriers of Christ's love in the slums. . . . We stand together holding the same chalice and so with the adoring angels satiate Christ's thirst for souls.

"How happy I am to have you all. You belong to me as much as every sister belongs to me here. Often when the work is very hard, I think of each one of you, and tell God: *Look at my suffering children and for their love bless this work,* and it works immediately. So you see you are our treasure house."

THE SISTERS OF THE WORD

My third second self is a French priest, Father Georges Gorrée, who organizes the wing of the contemplatives who support the Missionaries of Charity by their prayers and penances. (Fr. Gorrée died in 1977.)

We have also the sisters of the word. They are a

contemplative branch. They have three hours of prayer at home and one hour in the church. Then daily two hours to go out and speak of Jesus. Not public speaking in the squares or street corners, just to speak of Jesus to people who want to listen. People are eager to listen to those who speak of our Lord.

I wish I could retire there among the sisters and just live a contemplative life, just be with Jesus.

The celebrations on the occasion of our Silver Jubilee in 1975 were somehow very tiring, but it was all wonderful. People prayed for us and with us, we thanked God for what he had done through the Missionaries of Charity.

The last days, we went every day to pray in some temple or church. The archbishop gave us permission to do so. We prayed with the Jews, the Armenians, the Anglicans, the Jains, the Sikhs, the Buddhists, the Hindus. It was extraordinary.

I believe in the need for and efficacy of baptism.

Some priests, imbued with modern ideas, tell me I am wrong. I answer them, "Let's not argue. You will not convince me and I shall not convince you."

So, we shall continue to baptize those who want to receive that sacrament.

Our best helpers are all the baptized poor who died and went straight to heaven. Our best helpers are the 40,000 inmates of our homes for the dying who *died with God* after making an act of perfect love for him, surrendering fully to his holy will. They now pray for us and for our work. That is what brings so much grace to our apostolate.

In Latin America many people have not seen a priest for several years, and so they ask the sisters to baptize their young children. What a cause of happiness for the sisters.

We may not preach Christ as we would like to, because we receive help from the government and from various agencies. So our hands are tied. You may preach because you receive no help from anybody. A government official told me, "Tell the truth, you would like me to become a Christian, you are praying for that?"

I answered him, "When you possess something really good you wish your friends to share it with you. Now, I think that Christ is the best thing in the world and I would like all men to know him and love him as I do. But faith in Christ is a gift of God, who gives it to whom he likes."

The gentleman went away satisfied.

"I'VE FOUND GOD"

One day, I was walking down the streets of London and I saw a man quite drunk. He was looking so sad and miserable!

I went right up to him and took his hand, shook it and asked, "How are you?" (My hand is always warm.) And he said, "Oh, after so long I feel the warmth of a human hand!"

And his face lit up. And his face was different.

I only want to say that small things, done in great love, bring joy and peace.

One day, a girl from a Paris university came to work in Calcutta. Her face was marked by worry, but after some weeks of work in the Home of the Dying, she came to me and said, "I have found God."

"Where?" I asked her. And she said to me, "I found him in the Home for the Dying."

"And what did you do?" I inquired.

"I sent a telegram to my parents saying I have found God."

Feel often during the day the need for prayer and take trouble to pray.

Prayer enlarges the heart until it is capable of containing God's gift of himself.

Ask and seek, and your heart will grow big enough to receive him and to keep him as your own.

Wherever God has put you, that is your vocation.

It is not what we do but how much love we put into it.

4. As Poor as the Poor

Two Kinds of Poverty

We receive everything free, we give everything free, purely for the love of God.

Our people, the poor people, are very great people. They give us much more, much joy in accepting us and the little things that we do for them.

Our life of poverty is as necessary as the work itself.

God always provides. He will always provide. Though we have no income, no salary, no grants, no church maintenance, yet we have never had to send anybody away because we didn't have.

I have never been in need, but I accept what people give me for the poor.

I need nothing for myself. I never refuse what people give. I accept whatever.

There must be a reason why some people can afford to live well. They must have worked for it. I only feel angry when I see waste, when I see people throwing away things that we could use.

There are two kinds of poverty.

We have the poverty of material things. (For example, in some places like India and Ethiopia, and in other places where the people are hungry, not only for bread: real hunger!)

But there is also a much deeper, much greater hunger. That is the hunger for love and that terrible loneliness of being unwanted, unloved, being abandoned by everybody. Such are some people that you find, people that are sleeping in the streets of London, Rome, or Madrid, even people who are found in their homes (they are often called shut-ins). Maybe there is that kind of unwantedness, that unloved feeling even in our homes! We may know somebody who is handicapped like that and nobody takes notice!

TODAY'S BIGGEST DISEASE

The biggest disease today is not leprosy or cancer or tuberculosis, but rather the feeling of being unwanted, uncared for, deserted by everybody. The greatest evil is the lack of love and charity, the terrible indifference towards one's neighbor who lives at the roadside, the victim of exploitation, corruption, poverty, and disease.

It is easy to think of the poverty far away and forget very quickly. Today a great disease is that feeling of terrible loneliness, the feeling of being unwanted, having forgotten what human joy is, what the human feeling is of being wanted or loved. I think this is found in very well-to-do families also.

We may not have people hungry for a plate of rice or for a piece of bread in New York City, but there is a tremendous hunger and a tremendous feeling of unwantedness everywhere. And that is really a very great poverty.

We don't expect hunger here today, in Western countries.

We don't expect, maybe, that terrible loneliness.

But everywhere today hunger is not only for a piece of bread, but hunger for God, hunger for love.

Nakedness is not only a stolen piece of cloth, but that human dignity which we have stolen away from our poor people. We treat them as good-for-nothing, as thieves, as lazy people.

We don't need publicity.

God's work has to be done in his own way, and he has his own ways and means of making our work known. You can see what has happened throughout the world and how the sisters have been accepted in places where nobody ever knew anything about them. They have been accepted where many other people find it difficult to live or to be. So I think this is God himself proving that it is his work.

TO SHARE WITH A PURE HEART

As for material means, we depend solely on divine providence.

We have never had to turn anybody away, because

there has always been one more bed, one more plate of rice, one more blanket to cover.

We take God at his word. We depend solely on divine providence that comes through to us to the love of the people.

God is taking care of his poor people through us. He has shown such thoughtfulness and kindness to our people in so many small details!

We have many reasons to take to ourselves what he has said, that we are more important to him than the birds of the air and the flowers of the garden.

If I wrote or spoke for hours and hours, I would be able to give thousands of proofs of the delicate kindness and thoughtfulness of God.

We deal with thousands of people and yet there has not been one occasion when we have had to say to somebody, "Very sorry, we don't have . . ."

In Calcutta, we cope with more than 20,000 people every day. (The day we don't cook, they don't eat.)

I can remember, one day a sister came and told me, "Mother, there is no more rice for Friday and Saturday. We will have to tell the people that we don't have it."

I was a little surprised because in all my years I had never heard that before.

On Friday morning, at about 9:00, a truck full of bread—thousands of loaves of bread!—arrived.

Nobody in Calcutta knew why the government closed the schools, but the schools were closed and all the bread was brought to us and for two days our people ate bread and bread and bread!

I knew why God closed the schools: He closed the schools because he wanted our people to know that they are more important than the grass, the birds and the flowers of the fields; they are special to him.

Those thousands of people had to know he loved them, he cared for them. This is a repeated evidence of tender love, of the tender thoughtfulness of God himself for his people.

A gentleman asked me, "What should we do to remove poverty from India?"

I answered, "When you and I learn to share with them . . ." (We cannot share unless our lives are filled with love of God, unless our hearts are pure.)

I think God is only allowing us to see that without him poverty and misery is only what we can produce.

People now are trying to prove that they can do things, that they don't need God in their lives, that they are all-powerful. And so, trying to do things without God, they are producing more and more misery and poverty.

I find the poverty in the West much more difficult, much greater than the poverty I meet in India, in Ethiopia and in the Middle East, which is a material poverty. For example, when a few months ago, before coming to Europe and America, I picked up a woman from the streets of Calcutta, dying of hunger, I had only to give her a plate of rice and I satisfied her hunger. But the lonely and the unwanted and the homeless, the shut-ins who are spending their lives in such terrible loneliness, who are known by the number of their room and not by their name! I think this is the greatest poverty that a human being cannot bear and accept and go through.

WITH THE EMPEROR OF ETHIOPIA

When we opened the house in New York City, Cardinal Terence Cooke was very anxious that he should give every month a maintenance for the sisters. (He loves the sisters.)

I didn't want to hurt him, but I didn't know how to explain to him that our services are purely for the love of God and that we cannot accept maintenance. I expressed it the only way I could, "Your Eminence, I don't think God is going to become bankrupt in New York City!"

And he has shown: it keeps coming and coming. I went to the United States without a dollar. I left with so many. I don't know how many there are.

Something beautiful has happened in Calcutta: the ICI, the English firm that has been working in India for many years, has given us a gift for our people of Calcutta: a very big property. We are making it into a wonderful home with the help of many people.

Now we are bringing the sick and the dying to this new place where there is a nice garden and a nice place for them and plenty of space. We will be able to take many more people there.

When I took the sisters to Ethiopia in 1973, the emperor asked me, "What are the sisters going to do here; what are they going to do?"

I said, "They will give the love and compassion of Jesus to your people."

He told me, "This is a new way. This is Christ's own way. Come!"

And today the sisters are there, doing that, only that part of the work: just feeding the hungry Christ, clothing the naked Christ, giving a home to the home-less Christ. To be able to do this work, to continue doing this work of that surrender to God, of that loving trust and cheerfulness, our sisters live a life of prayer and sacrifice.

The other day I went to Hyderabad to start a new foundation and a Hindu gentleman I had never seen before had given his own house completely as a gift: a gift to the sisters. He had it registered in our name and everything was completely free: a beautiful house with a garden, everything. This is happening more and more every day, everywhere.

We went to Guatemala during the earthquake in 1976. The sisters have been there ever since and they have come to love and to be loved. They told me something so beautiful about a man, a very poor man, in Guatemala who had been picked up from the streets of the city and brought to our home.

He was very sick, very disabled, very hungry, very helpless, but somehow, with the help of everybody, he got well again. He told the sisters, "I want to go out and leave this bed for somebody else who may need it as much as I needed it when I came here."

I believe now he is working outside. I don't think he earns much, but he is working and every time he gets a little money, he remembers the other disabled people who are in the home and he goes to see them. He always takes something for them. As little as he has, he brings something. This is the gift of our people!

"Now I Believe . . ."

The problem of starvation is great, but if we look at the problem it is not the answer. We must act, begin with one person: giving happiness and relief to that person is worth taking trouble.

One day we picked up a man from the streets of Calcutta. He was in a very terrible condition. We couldn't give him food as we knew he was a starvation case.

Next morning, we started giving him rice, and as he lifted the rice to his mouth with both hands, he expired.

The first Christians died for Jesus and they were recognised because they loved one another.

The world never needed more love than today: people are starving for love.

In one place I found out that the parents feed the first child to enable him to go to school. The rest of the children are kept sleeping so that they can be fed only once a day. Do we really know that?

The other day, one of our sisters was washing a leper covered with wounds.

A Muslim priest was standing by and said, "All these years I have believed that Jesus Christ is a prophet. But today I believe Jesus Christ is God if he is able to give such joy to this sister, enabling her to do her work with so much love!"

In our society, we take a fourth vow to give wholehearted and free service to the poorest of the poor. By that fourth vow, we have gone to those beautiful people who have nothing, who have no one, the sick, the dying, the crippled, the alcoholic, the lepers: demented people who have forgotten what human love is, what a human touch is, what a human smile is.

We meet this kind of people and give them free service.

We have no income, no government grant, no church maintenance: only divine providence.

We have dealt with thousands and thousands of poor, but we never had to send anybody away because we had nothing to give. There is always something. Jesus keeps his word: we are more important to his Father than the flowers and the grass and the birds.

This beautiful vow is so tender, though it is demanding. It keeps us close to the poor. The closer we are to them, the closer they are to him.

That is why I always repeat that we Missionaries of Charity are not social workers. We may be doing social work, but we are really contemplatives right at the heart of the world.

We are with Jesus twenty-four hours a day. We do everything for Jesus. We do it to Jesus.

Some months ago, a man was picked up from the streets of Melbourne, Australia.

An alcoholic, he had been for years in that condition. The sisters took him to the Home of Compassion that we have in Melbourne.

From the way they touched him, from the way the sisters took care of him, suddenly to him it was clear, "God loves me!"

After a few weeks he was relieved and left the Home of Compassion.

He never touched alcohol again. He went back to his family and to his children and to his job.

When he received his first salary, he came to the sisters and gave them money and said, "I want you to be the love of God to them as you have been to me!"

I always tell people, "I don't want your money from abundance. I don't want to relieve your conscience, but I want you to give until it hurts: to give because you want to share the poverty and the suffering of our poor."

I think this consciousness is happening more and more.

We have to thank God that the poor people are giving us more than we give to them.

It is a privilege for us to serve them, because in serving them we are really serving Christ himself who said, "I was hungry, I was naked, I was homeless, I was sick. . . . You did it to me."

5. I Love Children

A Child Is a Gift of God

If we have today so many unhappy and broken families, and if we have in the world so much unhappiness and so much suffering, I think it is because the mother is not in the home!

It is very painful to accept what is happening in Western countries: a child is destroyed by the fear of having too many children and having to feed it or to educate it.

I think they are the poorest people in the world, who do an act like that.

A child is a gift of God.

I feel that the poorest country is the country that has to kill the unborn child to be able to have extra things and extra pleasures. They are afraid to have to feed one more child!

In Calcutta we are trying to fight abortion by adoption. In India, actually, they may leave the child in the dustbin, they may leave him in a dark door, but they would never kill the child.

In Calcutta we have a home for crippled and unwanted children. (In other places we have similar homes too.)

Their parents often can't feed them. Sometimes because they are crippled also, because they are blind, because they are diseased, they don't want their children.

Often we pick them up with their own parents, who have to be taken to the Home for the Dying. In that home the sisters bring in the people from the streets, from the lanes, from the drains, from all over the city.

They are unwanted, uncared for, sick, and dying.

We go to them bringing all possible joy and also the material help of which they are deprived.

In our homes for street children, if the child is healthy, we try to get a family to adopt the child. Lately, we have had many Hindu families who are taking our children into their own homes and readily adopting them.

If the child is not adopted, then we get a sponsoring parent for his education. We have over 6,000 children who are being paid for in different schools to be educated. So their future is brighter and more beautiful.

"MOTHER, DON'T SAY THAT"

We in India don't have the difficulties the rich people have. Even our people don't have abortion.

The mother will give birth to the child and after

the birth she may put the child in the dustbin. (I have picked up many children from the dustbins!) But she will never kill it.

We are fighting abortion by adoption.

It is beautiful to see how God has blessed us. The government has given us full permission to give these children in adoption.

Our houses are always full of children.

It is beautiful to see in how many lives the joy and love of a child has brought unity and peace!

I have seen parents, mothers going without many things, even begging, to give their child what it needs.

I have seen a mother holding her handicapped child, because that child is her child; she had an understanding love for its suffering.

I remember there was a woman who had twelve children, and the first child was terribly disabled, terribly handicapped.

I cannot describe what the child was like, mentally or physically.

I offered to take that child to our home, where we have so many like it. But she started crying and she said to me, "Mother, don't say that, don't say that! She is to me and to my family the greatest gift of God. All our love is centered on her. Our lives would be empty if you take her from us."

This is an understanding love!

Some weeks back, at midnight, I heard a child's cry at our gate. When I went down, I saw this little one (I don't think he was more than seven years old!) and crying he said, "I went to my father and my father didn't want me."

And he crossed the road and went to his mother

and his mother didn't want him. "But you want me," he said.

That was the suffering of the child, the break of the family: the child was wanted neither by the father nor the mother.

Cases such as this we have so many! They are unwanted and uncared-for everywhere.

THE "UNTOUCHABLE" CHILDREN

I cannot remember now to what city I had gone, but I remember it was one where I did not see any children.

I missed the children very badly, and walking down the street I suddenly saw a cart pulled by a young mother.

I crossed the street just to see the child. To my terrible surprise, there was no child in the cart: there was a little dog.

The hunger in the heart of that mother had to be satisfied. So she took anything: because she did not have a child, she had to take up a dog.

In many places the child is neglected, but animals are cared for. Animals are given special food and special this and that.

I love dogs myself very much, but still I cannot bear seeing a dog instead of a child.

One of the abandoned children that we had in our *Sishu Bhavan* I gave to a very high-class and rich family.

After a few months, I heard that the child had become very sick and completely disabled. So I went to that family and said, "Give me back the child and I will give you a healthy child."

The father looked at me and said, "Take my life first, then take the child."

He loved the child from his heart!

In Calcutta, every night we send word to all the clinics, to all the police stations, to all the hospitals, "Please do not destroy the child: we'll take the child."

So our house is always full of children. (There is a joke in Calcutta: "Mother Teresa is always talking about family planning and about abortion, but she has certainly not practised this at all: every day she has more and more children.")

We really have many children in our home. Yet God has worked a miracle: even in India, every day we have one or two families who come to adopt a child. Many are from outside, but many are being adopted in India.

For us who live and work among Indians, this is the greatest miracle that could happen. According to the Indian social doctrine of castes, my children and myself and the sisters are untouchables: therefore, to take one of our children into a Hindu family is something unbelievable. However, they are really taking them, and according to Hindu law, a child adopted becomes like flesh and blood in a closer way than in no other country except in India.

This is one of the greatest miracles that God has worked. I remember when I told Mrs. Indira Gandhi what I was doing with the children. She said, "No, that is not possible!" I answered her, "But we are doing it. Then, it must be possible."

God has been tremendously wonderful to us: we always get plenty of parents who are hungry to give a home to a child, to give their love to a child.

THE BANGLADESH MISUSED GIRLS

We are doing a lot of natural family planning. We find street beggars and lepers and they say, "You people who have made the vow of chastity, you are the best people to teach us family planning."

(The people in Calcutta tease me very often, saying, "You are preaching family planning but you yourself are not planning your family at all, because your family is growing every day.")

Our Lord has been very good to us, because our children are being given for adoption very fast.

Mrs. Gandhi has passed a law stating that any family who has no children and much land, it should be taken from them. So the result was our children went like hot cakes to the best families. They were adopted according to the Hindu law by the best families and that was the miracle of it, because our children come under the classification of untouchables. (For a Brahman family, for a high-class family, to take a child like that represents a tremendous change in the life of our Indian people.)

When we were invited to Bangladesh to take care of the girls that were misused by the army, we had to open a children's home for them and there was a great difficulty because it was against the Muslim and the Hindu law to take back into society the girls who had been misused.

We were facing a very great difficulty, but when Mujib said that these girls were the heroines of the country, that they had fought for their purity, that they had fought for their country, their own parents came and took them. We found many young men who offered to marry them.

But some doctors came to do abortions on those girls.

I happened to be there at the time. There was a lady doctor who kept on saying that the unborn child is not a human being. I asked her this question, "If you were married and you were bearing a child in your womb, would it be a child or what?" Then very nicely she answered, "That's another question."

It was a terrible fight with those people. I told them, "Our girls were misused, they were forced, they didn't want sin, but what you are going to make them do, or help them to do, is to commit murder, and this will be with them for life. They will never forget that they as mothers have killed their children."

Thank God, the Bangladesh government understood that I would take care of the children, that I would not allow any of them to be aborted. So they got it in writing that only if a girl chose herself to have abortion, they could touch her: otherwise, nobody else could do it. So we were able to save many children and many girls.

The beautiful part was that it was proved later that those girls were forced into what they had done and they were called "the heroines of the country."

And so, of the forty children that we received, more than thirty went to Canada and other places in adoption into wonderful families. But many were accepted by their own families.

THE MEXICAN BOY

Today we hear of these terrible killings of the child: that's abortion.

I wonder what has happened in our human hearts. It's something unnatural. Something has been lost. Something has been broken.

I have said before and I repeat every time, "The greater destroyer of peace today is the destruction of the child, the killing of the child, the murdering of the child."

How a mother can do that is beyond human understanding.

I was watching a dog with a little puppy: because there were too many people moving about, the dog was afraid the little puppy might be hurt. The dog took the puppy away and hid the puppy.

This animal has that instinct of love to protect that little puppy. There was so much care, so much tenderness and watching everybody lest they do harm to the little animal.

I had an extraordinary experience in Mexico, where we have a home for children and for the dying.

In 1976, the president had invited the sisters, after building a beautiful house for the poor people.

Unluckily, an accident happened: a small child of seven years fell and hurt himself very badly.

We took the child to the hospital, but he died on the operation table.

There was so much excitement. We had to go to the police, to court.

There had to be so many examinations and so on.

I said to the sisters, "I will go myself to the hospital

and explain how things happened, to prove that it was a simple accident." I was at the hospital from 9:30 in the evening to 5:00 in the morning, sitting and waiting for all those formalities to be filled, to be able to take the child home.

I could not get it from my mind: there was so much noise, anxiety, confusion, examinations, and doctors!

I had to get two doctors from outside to sign a paper, but those two doctors were afraid to sign a simple accident form.

How strange and contradictory! There is no fear of signing forms for the deliberate killing of the child that goes on every hour of the day through abortion, or fear of being taken into court. Some doctors seem to take it for granted that, because they are medical professionals, they can destroy anything. But medicine is not just a profession. The work of a doctor is a consecrated life to the service for others, to put their love for God in the service of the sick. It is not just making money, it is not a business: it is a life of consecration, it is a vocation. God has chosen them to heal, to be his hands in healing, to be his love and compassion for the sick and suffering.

I was really so surprised that I had to spend so many hours in the hospital just waiting for that one paper from the doctors to say, "Yes, you can take the child."

A few days ago, a woman came to me, and she was crying.

I had never seen anybody crying like that: it was real, deep sorrow.

She said to me, "I've read what you have said about

abortion and I have aborted twice already: Will God forgive me?"

I said, "Yes, if you are sincere. You go to confession and your sins will be washed away by the absolution that you will receive. Only make sure that you are really sorry from your heart."

Then she said, "But I am not a Catholic."

I told her, "According to your religion, you still pray: I will ask God to forgive you."

Then she made such a wonderful act of contrition! By the time I had finished praying, she was a different being, fully relieved.

What a terrible suffering must be the knowledge of having killed, of having murdered one's own child!

A Hindu woman told me: "I had an abortion eight years ago. Until today, every time I see a child eight years old, I turn my head. I can't look at that child. Every year, when I see a child six, seven years old, I say, "Oh, my child would have been seven years old, he could be holding my hand."

Why does she say this? Because it is impossible to break the gift of God within us, the love that he has created in us.

6. The Poor Are Wonderful People

"WE'RE ONLY SISTERS"

Our poor are very great people, very lovable people.
We don't know them, that's why we can't love them.
And if we don't love them, we can't serve them.
That's why I beg you: try to find your poor here, first
in your own home. Don't allow anybody to be lonely,
to feel unwanted, unloved, but especially your own,
especially your neighbor.

We have a home for the alcoholics in Melbourne, a
home for homeless alcoholics.

One of them was very badly hurt by another. Then
I thought this would be a case for the police. So we
sent for the police and the police came and asked
that gentleman, "Who did that to you?"

He started telling all kinds of lies, but he wouldn't
tell the truth, he wouldn't give the name, and the
policeman had to go away without doing anything.

Then I asked him, "Why did you not tell the police
who did that to you?"

73

He looked at me and said, "His suffering is not going to lessen my suffering."

He hid the name of his brother to save him from suffering.

How beautiful and how great is the love of our people, and this is a continual miracle of love that's spread among our people. We call them poor, but they are rich in love!

Our novices in New York City are all dressed in white.

Once, while walking out, they met a man terribly drunk in the street.

They thought it was a good chance. "This is the one to whom we have to give the word of God," they thought.

But as soon as he saw them coming close to him, he said, "Go away! I'm not ready!"

The two sisters tried to approach him, saying, "We are only sisters."

He said, "Oh, no! You are two angels from heaven. God has taken me by the hand and I am not ready!"

Very beautiful! I think he was ready, because after some time he went and made his confession and made his peace with God.

He was quite a wonderful man!

There is no great difference in the reality of one country or another, because it is always people you meet everywhere. They may look different or be dressed differently, or may have a different education or position. But they are all the same. They are all people to be loved. They are all hungry for love.

A TERRIBLY COLD NIGHT IN LONDON

In Calcutta alone, we have picked up over 57,000 people from the streets.

They come to us, we pick them up, we bring them to our shelter. They die so beautifully with God!

Up to now, I have never seen or met, nor have the sisters seen, any man or woman who refuses to say "sorry" to God; refuses to say, "I love you, my God."

One morning, a well-to-do lady came to Mass with us. As she wept and wept, she was going through the torture of Gethsemane.

Why? Her children and her husband had left her. Her children have given up faith and are leading terrible lives.

We will never understand the suffering of that person, or of the hundreds and hundreds of families that are going through this agony every day.

That's why we need holy priests to come, like the angel went to Joseph, to explain, to help, to teach that God loves them.

The other day somebody asked me, "What would you advise the politicians?"

I never mix up in politics, but it came from my heart, "They don't spend enough time on their knees. I think they would be better politicians if they did. . . ."

This is what we need when we have to decide things for others.

Where God is, there is love. And where there is love, there is always service. Because we, as Christians, have been created for greater things: we have been created to be holy because we have been created in the image of God.

The first time I was in London, we went out at night. It was a terrible, cold night and we looked for the people in the streets.

There was an old man, a well-spoken man, shivering with cold. He was in front of me. In front of him there was another man: a Negro man with his coat open.

The Negro was protecting him from the cold. That gentleman was saying, "Take me, take me anywhere. I am longing to sleep between two sheets."

We looked around and we could see many others. But if, after all, there is only one, he is Jesus. He is the one that is hungry for love, for care.

Our "Listening" Co-workers

The other day I was walking down the street. A man walked up to me and said, "Are you Mother Teresa?" I answered, "Yes." He asked, "Please send some of your sisters to our house. I'm half-blind and my wife is nearly mental. We are simply longing to hear a human voice. We have everything except . . ."

When I sent the sisters there, they found that it was true. They had everything, but those two with no one to call their own were so lonely. Their sons and their daughters were quite possibly very far away from them. They are unwanted now, useless so to say, and so they must die of sheer loneliness.

In some places, like in England, we have co-workers composing small "listening groups." They go to people, ordinary old people's houses, and sit down with them and let them talk and talk. Very old people love to have somebody listen to them and let them talk and talk. Very old people love to have somebody listen to them even if they have to tell the story of thirty years ago.

To listen, when nobody else wants to listen, is a very beautiful thing.

All over the world there is so much suffering because the family is destroyed! It is the woman who guards the family's love and unity.

Every woman can be equal to men if we have brains and if we have money. But no man can become equal to women in love and in ability to show service.

I never forget what happened to our sisters in Rome, where we work with the shut-ins.

They go to the poor people's houses. (We clean the house and give them a bath, wash their clothes in the house and so on.)

The sisters found someone left in a terrible condition.

They cleaned the room and washed his clothes and gave him a good bath, but he never spoke a word.

The sisters kept on going but he never spoke.

After two days he told the sisters, "You have brought God in my life, bring father also."

They went to the parish priest and brought the priest. That man who never spoke, only that sentence he said, made his confession (he was a Catholic). He made his confession after sixty years, and next morning he died. He had a beautiful death!

I had a very sad experience in one country. The mother of the family had died and there was a number of children.

The husband could not raise the amount of money

he had to pay for the burial and for the whole ceremony.

The sisters went around begging, he sold whatever he had, but the woman's body had to remain in the house for three days, until everything was paid.

Our people very often don't remain unmarried because they want to commit sin or out of pleasure. Most of them remain unmarried or they live together because they cannot pay for their marriage fees. And their children remain unbaptized because they cannot pay.

"I Don't Need to Light the Lamp

In many places, our sisters have to work at night. They have to go out in the streets. But they always keep that bright happy smile as if everything is all right!

I often tell my sisters, "We should be angels of mercy and comfort. We should take the image of Christ as a friend of the little ones to the children of the slums. We should love the poor with the love of Christ, help them with his same help, give as he gives, serve as he serves, save as he saves."

We have a place in Australia. (As you know, many of the aborigines live there in very bad conditions!)

When we went around in that place, we found an old man in a most terrible condition.

I went in there and tried to talk to him and then I said to him, "Kindly allow me to clean your place and clean your bed and so on." He answered, "I'm all right!"

I said to him, "You will be more all right if I clean your place."

In the end he allowed me to do it and when I was in his room (I call it a room, but it was really not a room!), I noticed that he had a lamp, a very beautiful lamp but covered with dirt and dust. I said to him, "Do you not light the lamp?" And he said, "For whom? Nobody comes here. I never see anybody. Nobody comes to me. I don't need to light the lamp."

Then I asked him, "If the sisters come to you, will you light the lamp for them?" He answered, "Yes, I'd do it!"

So the sisters started going to him in the evening and he used to light the lamp.

Afterwards (he lived for more than two years), he sent word to me through the sisters and said, "Tell my friend, the light she lit in my life is still burning!"

That was such a small thing, but it was there in that darkness of the loneliness! A light was lit and that light kept on burning.

I'll never forget during the Bangladesh suffering: we had ten million people in and around Calcutta.

I asked the government of India to allow a number of other congregations to come to our aid, to help us, because we were working the whole time.

They allowed them to come: about fifteen or sixteen different sisters came to help us, and each one, on leaving Calcutta, said the same thing, "I have received much more than I have given and I can never be the same person again; because I have touched Christ, I have understood what love is. What it is to love and to be loved!"

When I see people suffer, I feel so helpless!

It's difficult, but the only way I find is to say, "God loves you."

I always connect this by saying to them, "It's a sign that you have come so close to Jesus on the cross that he can kiss you."

I remember I told this to a woman who was dying of cancer with her small children surrounding her.

I didn't know which was the greater agony: the agony of leaving the children, or the agony of her body.

I told her, "This is a sign that you have got so close to Jesus on the cross that he can share his passion with you, he can kiss you."

She joined her hands and said, "Mother, please tell Jesus to stop kissing me." She understood so beautifully!

THE MOTHER WHO DID KNOW

Once a man came to our house and he told me, "There is a Hindu family with about eight children who have not eaten for a long time."

So, I quickly took some rice for that evening and went to their family and I could see real hunger on the small faces of these children. Yet the mother had the courage to divide the rice into two portions and she went out.

When she came back, I asked her, "Where did you go? What did you do?" And she said, "They are hungry also!"

Who were *they?* A Muslim family next door with as many children. She knew that they were hungry.

What struck me most was that she *knew*, and because she *knew*, she gave until it hurt.

This is something so beautiful! This is living love! She gave until it hurt.

I did not bring more rice that night because I wanted them to enjoy the joy of giving, the joy of sharing.

You should have seen the faces of those little ones! They just understood what their mother did. Their faces were brightened up with smiles. When I came in, they looked hungry, they looked so miserable, but the act of their mother taught them what true love was.

Once a very rich Hindu lady came to see me. She sat down and said, "You know, Mother, I want to share in your work." (More and more people are saying that in India now.)

I said it was very wonderful. But she made a mistake and said, "You know, I love beautiful saris." (She had a most expensive sari of 800 rupees. Mine is only eight rupees; hers was 800 rupees.) And so she said, "I love beautiful and expensive saris. I go every month and buy a sari."

I prayed a little bit to our Lady to give her the right answer how she would share in the work. And I said, "I'd better begin with the sari. You know, next time, when you go to buy a sari, instead of buying a sari of 800 rupees, you buy a sari of 500 rupees and with the remaining 300 you buy saris for the poor people."

And so, the poor thing has come down to paying 100 for a sari. I have told her, "Please do not go below 100!"

She said it had changed her life. She has really understood sharing. And she has told me that she has received much more than she has given.

WITH THE PRESIDENT OF MEXICO

I have learned how to love with great love from a little child in Calcutta. Once, there was no sugar and I do not know how that little Hindu child four years old heard in the school that Mother Teresa had no sugar for her children.

He went home and told his parents, "I will not eat sugar for three days: I will give my sugar to Mother Teresa."

His parents had never been to our house before to give anything, but after three days they brought him. He was so small, and in his hand there was a little bottle of sugar. How much can a four-year-old child eat? But the amount he could have eaten for three days, he brought. He could scarcely pronounce my name, but yet he gave and the love he put in the giving was beautiful.

I learned from that little one that at the moment we give something to him, it becomes infinite!

A young boy we had picked up had lost his mother who had died in our Home for the Dying. She had been of a good family, but had come down in life.

The boy grew up and wanted to become a priest. When he was asked, "Why do you want to become a priest?", he gave a very simple answer, "I want to do to other children what Mother Teresa has done for me: I want to love as she loved me, I want to serve as she served me."

Today he is a priest and a wonderful lover of all those who have nothing, who have no one, who are wanted by no one, of people who have forgotten what human love is, what a human touch is, what even a smile is.

I ask for holy priests to be like angels in our disturbed families, in our suffering families, because I think that the passion of Christ is being relived in our homes!

The president of Mexico sent for me. I told him that he had to become holy as a president: not a Missionary of Charity, but as a president.

He looked at me a bit surprised, but it is like that: we have to become holy, each of us, in the place where God has put us.

There are some wonderful things we learn from the poor people, especially from the poor people who have nothing, who are hungry, who are sick, who are absolutely nothing, but who have each other.

One day I picked up a child from the street. He was very hungry: God knows for how many days the child had not eaten!

Its little eyes were shining with hunger. (It's difficult for you and me to understand what hunger is.)

I gave him a piece of bread. The child started to eat that bread bit by bit.

I said to him, "Eat, eat the bread: I will give you more when you finish." That little one answered, "I am afraid when the bread is finished I will be hungry again." (That little one, so small, had already experienced hunger!)

We had him in our Children's Home. He had a nice bath and all that. We gave him nice clothes.

In the afternoon, the child disappeared. We ran after him and brought him back, but the child disappeared again.

I told the sisters, "Try to keep all the time with the child: not so close, but just watch where he goes and why he runs away and does not want to stay in the house."

Again the child ran away. A sister followed him and she found the child under a tree in a street. His mother was there. She was cooking something. God knows what he had picked up from the dustbin, but she was cooking something and the love and the joy between that mother and the child was something unforgettable.

Even though the food we give to our people is the best we have, yet that child said, "I'll go home. This is my home."

There was nothing there. Just a torn mat: no pillow, no blanket, nothing, under a tree in the street. And yet that child liked the home because of all the tenderness of his mother. The mother felt all the love for the child and they could live like that because they were in love with each other.

THE POOR ARE GREAT PEOPLE

I visited a home, one of the best homes in England. (Our sisters are there, working.) At that special home I went to visit, there were old people. I have never seen so many beautiful things and so many wonderful things in a home like I saw in that one. And yet, there was not a single smile on the faces of those people. All they were doing was looking towards the door!

I asked the sister in charge, "Sister, why are they like that, why are they not smiling?" (I'm used to seeing smiles on people's faces: because I think smiles generate smiles, just as love generates love.)

The sister answered, "It is like this every day. They're always waiting for somebody to come and visit them. Their loneliness is eating them up. And for days after days, they keep on looking. Nobody turns up!"

That unwantedness is great poverty!

Some time ago a big group of professors from the United States came to our house in Calcutta. Before leaving, they said to me, "Tell us something that will help us, that will help us to become holy."

And I said to them, "Smile at each other." (Because we have no time even to look at each other.) And one of them asked me, "Are you married, Mother Teresa?"

I said, "Yes, and I find it sometimes very difficult to smile at Jesus for he can be very demanding!"

I will give you an example of what hunger is.

A child got a piece of bread from a sister. (She had not eaten for some time.) I saw the child eating the bread crumb by crumb.

I said to her, "I know you are hungry: why don't you eat the bread?"

The little one answered, "I want it to last longer!"

She was afraid that with the bread finished her hunger would come again. And so she ate it crumb by crumb.

There was another child next to her. She was not eating. I thought she had finished the bread, but the little one said, "My father is sick. I am very hungry, but my father is sick and I think he would love to have this piece of bread."

That good little one was ready to go without food to be able to give the joy of that little piece of bread to her father.

The poor are great people. They don't need our sympathy. They don't need our pity.

They are great people!

They are our very lovable people!

7. Caring for the Lepers

SHANTINAGAR—TOWN OF PEACE

We have sisters who have been trained to take care of the lepers.

We take all the precautions possible to protect ourselves, to protect the sisters.

When they are properly trained, there is very little possibility of infection. But we are all—we must be! —ready, if it is God's will, that some sister will get it.

We have many, many lepers to look after. When we ask our young sisters who would like to go and work with the lepers, every hand is up.

You would be surprised: though they are so disfigured and so difficult to look at, yet every sister sees Christ in them.

We have thousands of lepers. They are so great, they are so beautiful in their disfigurement!

In Calcutta, we give them a Christmas party every year.

Last Christmas I went to them and I told them that

what they have is the gift of God, that God has a very special love for them, that they are very dear to him, that what they have is not a sin.

An old man who was completely disfigured, tried to come near to me and he said, "Repeat that once more. It did me good. I have always heard that nobody loves us. It is wonderful to know that God loves us. Please say that again!"

With the money and the car that the Holy Father Paul VI gave to me (we raffled the car), with that money we have built a rehabilitation center for lepers called Shantinagar (Town of Peace). There we train lepers and try to return them to a normal citizen's life.

In Calcutta alone, we have over 17,000 lepers to take care of, but altogether they are about 47,000.

We try to teach them to do things so that they can lead a normal life.

The greatest suffering for the lepers is that they are shunned by everybody, wanted by no one.

We try to bring new life to them.

We try curing them and we have had the most wonderful results. Many of them are completely cured. (If they come in time, they can be completely healed.)

We have mobile clinics all over the cities where we work. In India we have about sixty centers where the sisters are working with mobile clinics.

We give the lepers tender love and care.

We are in very close contact with them.

We try to have rehabilitation centers all over the country.

We want them to feel that they are really loved and wanted, that we are not afraid of them.

Of course, we segregate them, but without them being frightened of segregation.

We are dealing with more than 55,000 leprosy patients only in India, and with the help of the government we are creating rehabilitation centers for them.

As all people know, right from the beginning, from the time of Jesus, lepers were not accepted by anybody. They had to hide in graves and run away from everybody and ring a bell as they were passing by for people to stay away.

Today, the love for Jesus is bringing more and more people towards them.

Our numbers keep growing: more and more lepers are beginning to realize that there is somebody who loves them, somebody who wants them.

In these leprosy centers where we are looking after all the lepers, we are building a Child's Home.

The miracle of God is that the child born of leprosy patients is at its birth perfectly clean, perfectly healthy.

Before the child is born, we prepare the parents to give it up for the sake of its future.

They must give it straight away before they even kiss the child, before they start feeding the child.

We take care of the child.

One day, I saw a mother and a father lay their newborn baby of three days between them. They put the baby between them and each one looked at the little one, their hands going close to the child and then withdrawing, trying, wanting to kiss the child and again falling back.

I cannot forget the deep love of that father and mother for their little child.

I took the child and I could see the father and mother as I was walking.

I held the child towards them and they kept on looking until I disappeared from their eyes.

The agony and the pain it caused!

It hurt them to give up the child, but because they loved the child more than they loved themselves, they gave it up.

They are allowed to see the child, but they are not allowed to touch him.

It is beautiful to see that big sacrifice that our leper parents have to make for the sake of their children, so that the children will not be infected!

THE AMOUNT OF LOVE

Some years back, the government in Calcutta decided to sterilise every leprosy family.

Feeling as a member of that group, I fought and said, "I will teach them natural family planning. I will take every newborn child, but you have no right to destroy what God has so beautifully created in every human being."

Thank God, they didn't do it.

So, now we are taking care of those 55,000 lepers and the government gives us land in every state to rehabilitate them and in every place we have a home for the children.

The sisters who teach the leprosy family, we call "educators."

It is so beautiful to see them in the evening sitting together with this leprosy family, teaching them the natural family planning: how to plan their family, without committing sin.

A group of lepers, of slum dwellers, of beggars (these are our people!) came to the house one day to thank me for allowing the young sisters, the novices, to teach them this family planning.

They said, "You people who have a vow of chastity, you are the best people to teach us because it is nothing else but self-control out of love for each other. We thank you for teaching us because our family is united, our family is healthy and we can have a baby whenever we want."

We have heard the government say that in these years more than 150,000 less babies have been born in Calcutta alone, because of this beautiful way among the beggars, among the lepers, among the slum dwellers.

It is beautiful to see them: how they help each other to grow in love!

A few weeks back, one of our brothers came to me in distress and said, "My vocation is to work for the lepers. (He loves the lepers.) I want to spend all my life, my everything in this vocation."

I said to him, "You are making a mistake, brother. Your vocation is to belong to Jesus. He has chosen you for himself and the work is only a means of your love for him in action. Therefore it does not matter what work you are doing, but the main thing is that you belong to him, that you are his and that he gives you the means to do this for him."

So for all of us, it doesn't matter what we do or where we are as long as we remember that we belong to him, that we are his, that we are in love with him.

The means he gives us, whether we are working for the rich or we are working for the poor, whether we are working with high-class people or low-class people, it makes no difference; but how much love we are putting into the work we do is what matters.

OUR NOT-CHRISTIAN CO-WORKERS

One Hindu gentleman, the head of a religious group, said at a meeting that looking at the sisters and their work when they are serving the poor people and especially the lepers, he feels that Christ has come once more on this earth and he is going about doing good.

Another Hindu gentleman, who came to the Home for the Dying, said, "Your religion must be true. Christ must be true if he helps you to do what you're doing."

And that is: we preach Christ without preaching. Not by words, but by putting his love and our love into a living action of serving the people in their needs; by loving and serving the dying, the homeless, the abandoned destitute, the lepers.

That part of the work has been very beautiful.

The work itself is not very great: many people are doing the same work. But it has created a concern and awakening that the poor are our brothers and sisters and they have been created by the same loving hand. That oneness is more and more coming into reality.

People are beginning to get more concerned and more anxious to share their help. In Calcutta, for example, we have many more people now, who are not Christians (Christians too, but majority are not Christians), who come on a regular basis just to do the humble work: to wash, to wash clothes, to cook meals, to feed the people.

On special occasions, when they have their anniversary or something like that, they come themselves and feed the people with their hands.

This was unheard of before in places like India.

Very often I ask people to come to our Home for the Dying in Calcutta. I ask them not to come and give things (things I can get for the asking).

I want them there so that they see the dying: to smile at them, to be with them.

It means such a lot to our people!

8. Our Home for the Dying

DEATH IS BEAUTIFUL

I am very sure that all those people who have died with us are in heaven. They are really saints. They are in the presence of God.

It may be that they were not wanted on this earth but they are very beloved children of God.

I would like you to pray and to thank God for all the beautiful things our sisters have done in the Home for the Dying.

Death is something beautiful: it means going home.

Naturally, we feel lonely for that person. But it is a very beautiful thing: a person has gone home to God.

My first contact with the dying destitute was like this: One day, while seeking for the poor, I saw and picked up the first person from the streets.

I found a woman dying in the street, eaten up by rats. I took her to the nearest hospital, but the people there didn't seem to want her there.

In the end, because I insisted so much, they took her in.

From then on, I decided to find a place for them myself and take care of them.

I went to the municipality and I asked only for a place; the rest I would do myself.

They took me to the Kali temple in Kalighat and offered me a place of rest that they used for pilgrims that come to worship the Goddess.

We have continued there for many years and we have picked up thousands of people from the streets of Calcutta.

One day I picked up a man from an open drain. Except for his face, his whole body was full of wounds.

I brought him to our house. (We have a Home for the Dying near the temple of the Goddess Kali, the goddess of fear and destruction, right there in the temple.) And what did that man say? "I have lived like an animal in the street, but I am going to die like an angel, loved and cared for."

We just had time to give him a bath and clean him and put him in bed. After three hours, he died with a big smile in his face and with a ticket for Saint Peter. (Saint Peter will not let them go inside heaven without that ticket.) We gave him a special blessing by which his sins were forgiven—whatever sins he had ever committed—and he could see the face of God for all eternity. There was no complaint, there was no cursing, there was no fear.

In twenty-five years we have picked up from the streets of Calcutta alone 36,000 people, of which 17,000 have died a beautiful death, with a ticket for Saint Peter.

SHE COULDN'T BELIEVE IT WAS RICE

I picked up a woman from a dustbin and she was burning with fever. She was in her last days and she kept saying, "My son did this to me!"

I picked her out and took her home, then I brought her to the convent. On the way I tried to make her accept; to forgive her son.

It took me a long time to make her say, "I forgive my son." Just before she died, she was able to say that with a real forgiveness.

But she was not concerned that she was dying. She was not concerned that she was burning with fever. She was not concerned that she was suffering so much.

The breaking of the heart was that her son did not want her.

I think that this is something that you and I must understand.

One night in Calcutta we picked up some patients from the street.

One of them was in very bad condition. I told the sisters, "I will take care of her and you take care of the other three."

She was actually eaten alive with worms and maggots.

I took care of her and all that my love could have done I did for her.

When I put her in bed, she took hold of my hand. There was a beautiful smile. I have never seen a smile like that on a human face! There was a beautiful smile on her face and she said one word only, "Thank you!" And she died.

For a second, I reflected, looking at her and said, "If I was her, what would I have done?"

My sincere answer was, "I would have tried to draw attention to myself. I would have said, *I'm cold!*, or *I'm hungry!*, or *I'm dying,* or something. But this wonderful woman, she gave me more than I gave to her. She gave me her understanding love."

These are our people!

Do we know them? They may be in our homes. The lonely people are everywhere: do we know them?

We have homes for the dying in many places.

One day I picked up a woman from the street. I knew she was dying of hunger. I gave her a plate of rice, and she kept on looking at the rice.

I tried to ask her to eat. Then she said just very simply, in a very ordinary way, "I haven't . . . I can't believe it's rice. For a long time I have not eaten!"

She didn't blame anybody. She didn't even blame the rich. She just couldn't believe it was rice!

The poor are great people!

We must love them, not by feeling pity for them. We must love them because it is Jesus in the distressing disguise of the poor.

They are our brothers and sisters.

They are our people.

Those lepers, those dying, those hungry, those naked: they are Jesus!

HOME TO GOD!

I have never felt ashamed to look at the cross until one day when a young woman came with her child in her hands.

She said to me she had gone to two or three different convents asking for a little bit of milk for her child.

She was answered, "You are lazy. Go and work!" and so on.

By the time she came to our house, when I took the child it died in my hands.

I felt ashamed to look at the cross because Jesus has given us so much and we could not give even a glass of milk to this little child.

The other day some sisters were telling me that in one place they went they were told that a person had died in her room God knows when.

They broke open the door and what did they find there? The rats were eating the body!

They tried to find out who she was, what she was, whose child she was. Whose mother was she? Whose wife was she?

Nobody!

They all knew her by the number of her room. Even the next-door neighbor didn't know her.

This is terrible poverty: loneliness, fear, that feeling of being unwanted, unloved, uncared for.

This is what we must remove from our families.

Our Home for the Dying is the home for the homeless Christ. Our hungry people are the hungry Christ.

I remember that at the beginning of my work I had

a very high fever and in that delirious fever I went before Saint Peter.

He said to me, "Go back! There are no slums in heaven!"

So I got very angry with him and I said, "Very well! Then, I will fill heaven with slum people and you will have slums then!"

When somebody dies, that person has gone home to God. That's where we all have to go.

9. My Spiritual Principles

MY LIFE AND MY FAITH

The meaning of my life is the love of God.

It is Christ in his distressing disguise whom I love and serve.

Jesus has said, "I was hungry and you gave me to eat; I was naked and you clothed me; I was homeless and you took me in . . ."

Nobody can take my religion from me. Therefore, nobody can refuse me to the right to practice it.

Nobody can take it away from me. It is something within me. If there is no alternative to persecution and if that is the only way that Christ wants to come among his people, by radiating his love for them through my actions, I would stay to serve them, but I wouldn't give up my faith.

I would be ready to give my life, but not my faith.

I am nothing. He is all. I do nothing of my own. He does it.

That is what I am, God's pencil. A tiny bit of pencil with which he writes what he likes.

God writes through us, and however imperfect instruments we may be, he writes beautifully.

To Ignore the Poor Is to Ignore Christ

I have loved Jesus with my whole heart, with my whole being.

I have given him all, even my sins and he has espoused me to himself in tenderness and love.

Now and for life I am the spouse of my crucified spouse.

I have accepted the responsibility of representing the poor of the world: the unwanted, the unloved, the uncared for, the crippled, the blind, the lepers, the alcoholics, the people thrown away by society, people who have forgotten what human love is or what the human touch is.

I have come to realize more and more that the greatest disease and the greatest suffering is to be unwanted, unloved, uncared for, to be shunned by everybody, to be just nobody to no one.

I try to give to the poor people for love what the rich could get for money.

I wouldn't touch a leper for a thousand pounds. Yet I willingly cure him for the love of God.

When I see how the poor remain neglected and unrecognized all around us, I understand the sadness of Christ at not being accepted by his own. Today those who ignore or reject the poor, ignore or reject Christ.

The poor do us the honor of allowing us to serve them.

OUR WAY TO SERVE GOD

The Mass is the spiritual food which sustains me, without which I could not get through one single day or hour in my life. In the Mass we have Jesus in the appearance of bread, while in the slums we see Christ and touch him in the broken bodies and in the abandoned children.

At times, I feel rather sad, because we do so little. Most people praise us for our actions, but what we do is not more than a drop of water in the ocean. It hardly affects the immensity of human suffering.

If there are people who feel that God wants them to change the structure of society, that is something between them and their God. We must serve him in whatever way we are called.

I am called to help the individual, to love each poor person, not to deal with institutions. I am in no position to judge.

In the Eucharist I see Christ in the appearance of bread.

In the slums, I see Christ in the distressing disguise of the poor.

The Eucharist and the poor are but one love for me.

Only in heaven we will see how much we owe to the poor for helping us to love God better because of them.

It is easy to love the people far away.

It is easier to give a cup of rice than to relieve the loneliness and pain of someone unloved in our own home.

THE MIRACLE OF OUR HAPPINESS

Our people are poor by force, but our poverty is of our own choice. We want to be poor like Christ who, being rich, chose to be born and live and work among the poor.

Our constitutions state: "We and our poor will rely entirely on divine providence. We are not ashamed to beg from door to door as members of Christ, who himself lived on alms during the public life and whom we serve in the sick and the poor."

If the society is God's work, it will endure. But if the sisters are not to be faithful, if they are not to work for God's glory, then God may as well suppress the society.

The miracle is not that we do this work, but that we are happy to do it.

We do nothing. He does everything. All glory must be returned to him.

God has not called me to be successful.

He called me to be faithful.

God made me a great gift: good health.

SIMPLY A SHADOW

One of my favorite devotional songs is called Only a Shadow. Its verses run like this:

The love I have for you, my Lord,
Is only a shadow of your love for me,
Your deep abiding love.
My own belief in you, my Lord,
Is only a shadow of your faith in me,
Your deep and trusting faith.
My life is in your hands.
My love for you will grow, my Lord.
Your light in me will shine.
The dream I have today, my Lord.
Is only a shadow of your dream for me,
If I but follow you.
The joy I feel today, my Lord,
Is only a shadow of your joys for me,
Only a shadow of all that will be
When we meet face to face.

To me, to be a Christian is very important. To me it means everything, because each individual has to act according to the grace God gives to his soul.

God gives to every soul that he has created a chance to come face to face with him, to accept him or to reject him.

God has his own ways and means to work in the hearts of men and we do not know how close they are to him. But by their actions we will always know whether they are at his disposal or not.

How you live your life is the proof that you are or not fully his, whether one is a Hindu or a Moslem or a Christian.

In India I was asked by some government people, "Don't you want to make us all Christians?"

I said, "Naturally. The treasure I have, I want to

give to you, but I cannot. I can pray for you that you may have the courage to receive it, because faith is a gift of God, that great gift of God that he has given to us in holy communion, to satisfy our hunger, because we have been created in the image of God."

All my time belongs to others.

This also happens with the sisters.

They work without rest for the ill and for the children. They do not have time even to write a letter.

I say to all those that write to us, "Don't become offended if you do not receive an answer: our work is really big and we do not have time left to write letters."

THE ANGELUS BELL

In many places the poor are happy to hear the Angelus bell. In New York City the poor complained to the sisters, "Why is it that we don't hear the Angelus now? We were happy to pray to our Lady when we heard the bell rung, the announcement of the good news of the coming of the Savior."

The sisters asked the priest, who said he had no time to ring the bell three times a day, and the parish could not afford to pay a person to come and ring it. So the sisters took up the duty. "We shall come and ring, father," they said. And now the poor of that very difficult locality are happy that they can again pray the Angelus.

The poor are hungry for God; they want to hear about our Lord. They do not worry so much about material things; they want to hear that they have a father in heaven who loves them.

It is very difficult to give Jesus to the people unless we have Jesus in our hearts.

We all should become the carriers of God's love. But to do this, we must deepen our life of love and prayer and sacrifice.

We must bring peace, love and compassion to the world today. We don't need guns and bombs to do this. We need deep love, deep union with Christ to be able to give him to others.

Compassion and love have to grow from within, from our union with Christ.

And from that union, love for the family, love for the neighbor, love for the poor is a natural fruit.

So let us deepen our love for Jesus, deepen our knowledge of God, and this knowledge will lead us to love him, and love will lead us to serve him as instruments of peace, of love, of compassion.

We need to find God, and he cannot be found in noise and restlessness.

God is the friend of silence.

See how nature—trees, flowers, grass—grows in silence.

See the stars, the moon, and the sun, how they move in silence.

Is not our mission to give God to the poor in the slums?

Not a dead God, but a living, loving God.

The more we receive in silent prayer, the more we can give in our active life.

We need silence to be able to touch souls.

The essential thing is not what we say, but what God says to us and through us.

All our words will be useless unless they come from within.

Words which do not give the light of Christ increase the darkness.

SILENCE AND KINDNESS

Man needs silence.

To be alone or together looking for God in silence.

There it is that we accumulate the inward power which we distribute in action, put in the smallest duty and spend in the severest hardships that befall on us.

Silence came before creation, and the heavens were spread without a word.

Christ was born in the dead of night; and though there has been no power like his, "He did not strive nor cry, neither was his voice heard in the streets."

Once I was asked by someone what I consider most important in the training of the sisters. I answered:

Silence. Interior and exterior silence. Silence is essential in a religious house. The silence of humility, of charity, the silence of the eyes, of the ears, of the tongue. There is no life of prayer without silence.

Silence, and then kindness, charity; silence leads to charity, charity to humility. Charity among themselves, accepting one another when they are different; charity for union in a community. Charity leads to humility. We must be humble. It strikes me how

God is humble. He humbled himself. He who possessed the fullness of the Godhead took the form of a servant. Even today God shows his humility by making use of instruments as deficient as we are, weak, imperfect, inadequate instruments.

Then, there must be joy in the heart, the joy of serving God, the joy of doing his work. That is not incompatible with humility.

Indeed, in her Magnificat, Mary exclaimed that she rejoiced because "He who is mighty has done great things to me!"

Yes, I tell the sisters not to fear to do good before the eyes of men. Our Lord said, "Let your light shine before men, that seeing your good deeds they may praise your Father in heaven!" So, let men see your good deeds: it is Christ who does them through you.

When people praise us for what we are doing, I do not mind it at all. Rather, I rejoice because it all leads to the glory of God.

TALKING WITH MALCOLM MUGGERIDGE

More and more often, I am requested to speak in public. This is an ordeal for me. I wish I did not have to do it.

I close my eyes and let him speak. I follow Jesus' inspiration.

While I am speaking, I don't look at my audience.

I look straight in front of me, above their heads. I look at no one. I deliver my message.

I gave a BBC interview.

Malcolm Muggeridge had asked me to appear on

one of his programs. That was the first time I appeared on TV. They received me at the studio and led me into a small room with a table and two chairs. I sat on one of the chairs and started saying my rosary.

After some time, Mr. Muggeridge arrived, sat down in front of me, and started asking me questions. He had a paper with a list of questions before him. He read two of them which I answered; then I went on talking about what I wanted to say.

While I spoke, they were taking pictures of me. But I did not care; I just went on talking, looking straight in front of me, without moving my head.

Trust God.
  Feel the security of divine providence.
  Trust him.
  He knows.
  He will provide.
  Let him test and trust our faith in him.
  Wait on him.
  Trust and believe.

HOLINESS AND SUFFERING

Become holy.
  This is my prayer each day for you.
  The way to holiness is prayer.
  We must believe and bring our faith into reality and life by love.
  Begin at home.
  It's harder to love at home than to love those outside.
  Love.

Love Jesus in people.

Serve him in them.

Love until it hurts.

Real love is always painful and hurts: then it is real and pure.

Prayer is simply talking to God.

He speaks to us: we listen.

We speak to him: he listens.

A two-way process: speaking and listening.

Say this prayer often: "Jesus, in my heart, I believe in your tender love for me. I love you."

The more you pray, the easier it becomes.

The easier it becomes, the more you'll pray.

Ask your priests to teach you to pray: worry them to teach you. Say the *Our father* slowly. Pray at home every day even if it is only for five minutes.

Teach your family to be aware of the poor.

Encourage them to go and do something for so many who are in need, for so many who are starving.

Live simply.

Give example through simplicity.

The spirit of poverty is dependency on God.

Trust him.

Be with and love the poorest of the poor.

You can and you must expect suffering.

It is a sign that Jesus is near when you are suffering.

Jesus is very near, watching you.

Suffering empties us out for Jesus.

MONEY'S NEVER A PROBLEM

Saint Teresa of Avila? Oh, no! I haven't called myself after the big Teresa, but after the little one, Teresa of Lisieux.

Without our suffering, our work would just be social work: very good and helpful, but it would not be the work of Jesus Christ, not part of the redemption.

Jesus wanted to help by sharing our life, our loneliness, our agony, our death. Only by being one with us has he redeemed us.

We are asked to do the same: all the desolation of the poor people, not only their spiritual destitution, must be redeemed. And we must share it, for only by being one with them can we redeem them; that is, by bringing God into their lives and bringing them to God.

There are times when I feel absolutely empty; an empty shell; a thing without substance, with nothing in me to support me I feel so lonely and miserable.

Each time I go to Europe and America, I am struck by the unhappiness of so many people living in those rich countries: so many broken homes; children not looked after by their parents. Their first duty is to work among their own people, bring together separated couples, build good homes where the children may receive their parents' love.

They have material wealth; they lack spiritual values.

Money? I never give it a thought. It always comes. We do all our work for our Lord; he must look after us. If he wants something to be done, he must give us the means. If he does not provide us with the means, then it shows that he does not want that particular work. I forget about it.

JESUS TO ME

This is Jesus to me:
   The Word made flesh.
   The Bread of life.
   The Victim offered for our sins on the cross.
   The Sacrifice offered at the Holy Mass for the
      sins of the world and mine.
   The Word—to be spoken.
   The Truth—to be told.
   The Way—to be walked.
   The Light—to be lit.
   The Life—to be lived.
   The Love—to be loved.
   The Joy—to be shared.
   The Sacrifice—to be offered.
   The Peace—to be given.
   The Bread of life—to be eaten.
   The Hungry—to be fed.
   The Thirsty—to be satiated.
   The Naked—to be clothed.
   The Homeless—to be taken in.
   The Sick—to be healed.
   The Lonely—to be loved.
   The Unwanted—to be wanted.
   The Leper—to wash his wounds.
   The Beggar—to give him a smile.
   The Drunkard—to listen to him.
   The Mental—to protect him.
   The Little One—to embrace him.
   The Blind—to lead him.
   The Dumb—to speak for him.
   The Crippled—to walk with him.

The Drug Addict—to befriend him.
The Prostitute—to remove from danger and be-
friend her.
The Prisoner—to be visited.
The Old—to be served.

To me Jesus is my God.
Jesus is my Spouse.
Jesus is my Life.
Jesus is my only Love.
Jesus is my All in all.
Jesus is my Everything.

About the Editors

Editors José Luis González-Balado and Janet N. Playfoot
have long been involved in the work of Mother Teresa
and have drawn the material for this book from a world-
wide network of co-workers who have collected and
recorded Mother Teresa's words over the years. José
Luis González-Balado is a specialist in religious biogra-
phies and has published ones on Pope Paul VI, Brother
Roger of Taize, and Ernesto Cardenal. His wife, Janet
N. Playfoot, is a social worker and teacher who collabo-
rates with her husband in his writing and in helping
Mother Teresa's work in Spain.